SIMPLY JOYCE

SIMPLY JOYCE

MARGOT NORRIS

Simply Charly
New York

First Edition 2016

Cover Illustration by José Ramos
Cover Design by Scarlett Rugers

Simply Charly
5 Columbus Circle, 8th Fl
New York, NY 10019
www.simplycharly.com

ISBN: 978-1-943657-11-7

Contents

Praise for *Simply Joyce*

"*Simply Joyce* is a perfect introduction to the complex work of one of the foremost writers of the twentieth century. Margot Norris, who has devoted her professional life to opening Joyce's canon to all levels of readers, has produced a lucid, erudite, and entertaining overview that will engage those who have heretofore been intimidated by Joyce's reputation and will revive in others a recollection of the pleasures that have derived from his writing. Although Norris offers a compact overview, it is by no means reductive or simplistic. Rather, in deft but accessible language, she lays out the marvelous range of possible responses to Joyce's work. Her book is a wonderful gift to all readers who love Joyce's writing."

—Michael Patrick Gillespie, Professor of English and Director of the Center for the Humanities in an Urban Environment at Florida International University

"This new book by Margot Norris, one of the world's leading James Joyce scholars, is a remarkably thorough and yet concise introduction to Joyce and his four major works. Norris's commentaries on Joyce's language are particularly useful, and as she works her way from *Dubliners* to *A Portrait of the Artist as a Young Man*, *Ulysses*, and *Finnegans Wake*, she calls attention to crucial elements of each book, including their experiments with literary form and the values they embody."

—Patrick A. McCarthy, Professor of English, University of Miami and editor of the James Joyce Literary Supplement

"In *Simply Joyce*, Margot Norris, a world-renowned Joyce scholar, provides a succinct, enticing and informative overview of Joyce's works. Her dexterous accounts of his challenging texts underscore how they openly invite us to immerse ourselves in them and interpret them. She comprehensively introduces readers to the intricacies of all of Joyce's writings, including his fiction, poetry and his single surviving play, *Exiles*, at once taking stock of their fundamental structures and crisply commenting on them. Norris's engaging primer never shirks the difficulty of Joyce's masterpieces. But she triumphantly shows that the pleasures of reading Joyce are open to everyone, both novices and scholars alike."

—Anne Fogarty, Professor of James Joyce Studies, University College Dublin, Ireland

"*Simply Joyce* is a smart, sensible, clear, and useful introduction to the revolutionary and innovative—but also controversial and challenging—20-century masterworks by James Joyce."

—Vincent J. Cheng, Shirley Sutton Thomas Professor of English, University of Utah and author of *Joyce, Race, and Empire* and other studies

Other *Great Lives* Titles

Simply Austen by Joan Klingel Ray
Simply Beckett by Katherine Weiss
Simply Beethoven by Leon Plantinga
Simply Chaplin by David Sterrett
Simply Chopin by William Smialek
Simply Darwin by Michael Ruse
Simply Descartes by Kurt Smith
Simply Dirac by Helge Kragh
Simply Dostoevsky by Gary Saul Morson
Simply Edison by Paul Israel
Simply Eliot by Joseph Maddrey
Simply Euler by Robert E. Bradley
Simply Faulkner by Philip Weinstein
Simply Freud by Stephen Frosh
Simply Gödel by Richard Tieszen
Simply Hegel by Robert Wicks
Simply Heidegger by Mahon O'Brien
Simply Hemingway by Mark P. Ott
Simply Hitchcock by David Sterrett
Simply Machiavelli by Robert Fredona
Simply Napoleon by J. David Markham & Matthew Zarzeczny
Simply Nietzsche by Peter Kail
Simply Newton by Michael Nauenberg
Simply Riemann by Jeremy Gray
Simply Tolstoy by Donna Tussing Orwin
Simply Turing by Michael Olinick
Simply Twain by R. Kent Rasmussen
Simply Wagner by Thomas S. Grey
Simply Wittgenstein by James C. Klagge
Simply Woolf by Mary Ann Caws

Series Editor's Foreword

Simply Charly's "Great Lives" series offers brief but authoritative introductions to the world's most influential people—scientists, artists, writers, economists, and other historical figures whose contributions have had a meaningful and enduring impact on our society. Each book, presented in an engaging and accessible fashion, provides an illuminating look at their works, ideas, personal lives, and the legacies they left behind. Our authors are prominent scholars and other top experts who have dedicated their careers to exploring each facet of their subjects' work and personal lives.

Unlike many other works that are merely descriptions of the major milestones in a person's life, the "Great Lives" series goes above and beyond the standard format and content. Every book includes not just the biographical information, such as the little-known character traits, quirks, strengths and frailties, but, above all, focuses on each individual's extraordinary professional achievements.

In its exploration of famous lives that have sometimes been shrouded in secrecy, surrounded by myths and misconceptions, or caught up in controversies, the "Great Lives" series brings substance, depth, and clarity to the sometimes-complex lives and work of history's most powerful and influential people.

What can a reader learn from the "Great Lives" series? These volumes shed light on the thought processes, as well as specific events and experiences, that led these remarkable people to their groundbreaking discoveries or other achievements; the books also present various challenges they had to face and overcome to make history in their respective fields.

We hope that by exploring this series, readers will not only gain new knowledge and understanding of what drove these geniuses, but also find inspiration for their own lives. Isn't this what a great book is supposed to do?

Charles Carlini, Simply Charly
New York City

Preface

James Joyce is considered one of the most important and influential writers of the twentieth century. But is he one of the most widely read? This question is prompted by what many consider the extraordinary difficulty of some of his works, which daunted readers from the very beginning of their publication. The Irish writer George Moore was sent a copy of *Ulysses* shortly after it was published, and immediately complained about it. "I was told I must read it, but how can one plow through such stuff?" he told a friend. A century later these works remain difficult for many readers approaching them for the first time, and *Simply Joyce* has this readership particularly in mind as it offers discussion and analysis of Joyce's writing. The project of this book is not to simplify Joyce by putting aside the remarkable complexity that makes his themes and language so aesthetically and intellectually rich, but to make his unique work accessible. The approach that will enable this is to offer an introduction to Joyce's life and career, followed by a systematic study of each of his major works: the short stories of *Dubliners,* his coming-of-age novel *A Portrait of the Artist as a Young Man,* his classic *Ulysses*, and the highly experimental *Finnegans Wake.* Readers will be led through each of these works consecutively, from beginning to end, with descriptions and summaries of the themes, but also with attention to the language, not only to what it says but also to what it does not say, to its mode of expression, the often layered meanings of the words, the humor of its puns and double entendres, and the beauty of its sound. In the process, attention will focus on the surprisingly ordinary traits and circumstances of Joyce's numerous characters among the colorful population of Dublin, Ireland in the early 20th century: the thoughtful children at the beginning of *Dubliners*, the young artist of *Portrait* struggling with ambition and family poverty, the Jewish advertising canvasser and his outspoken wife in *Ulysses*, and the complicated men, women, and children in *Finnegans Wake*, who are not only humans but also rivers and landscapes, animals and clouds, and illuminating symbols. The challenge for *Simply Joyce* will be to present this rich array of literary life without losing sight of the aesthetic and intellectual complexities of the language in which it is vested.

Given the challenges posed by the four major works, and particularly *Ulysses* and *Finnegans Wake*, it may be helpful to ease into our discussion of Joyce's life and writings by noting that these ambitious texts were not Joyce's only accomplishments. He also produced a collection of poems, assorted insights or 'epiphanies', a series of critical essays, a notebook titled *Giacomo Joyce,* and a play called *Exiles*. These diverse writings do not share the fame of the later productions, but they have their merits and serve as a useful prelude to his more classical texts. Joyce's verses, in particular, have a lyrical quality, and the distinguished Irish poet W.B. Yeats appears to have found some of the early poems highly promising. They, therefore, function as an indicator of the poetic quality of Joyce's later prose, the way words are selected for the effects of their sounds and rhythms, creating a form of verbal music. Given his life-long love of music, it is not surprising that Joyce titled his first published collection of poetry "Chamber Music," although this title by one account was inspired by his listening to the sound of urine tinkling into a chamber pot.

The musical theme appears in the opening lines of the first poem: "Strings in the earth and air/ Make music sweet;/ Strings by the river where/ The willows meet" (*Collected Poems* 9). The music appears to be produced by "Love," a male figure wearing "Pale flowers on his mantle" and dark leaves in his hair, his head bent as his fingers are "straying/ Upon an instrument" (9). While Love plays a string instrument, a female figure in the next poem appears to be playing the "yellow keys" of an old piano, and in poem IV, there is the sound of singing:

> When the shy star goes forth in heaven
> All maidenly, disconsolate,
> Hear you amid the drowsy even
> One who is singing by your gate.
> His song is softer than the dew
> And he is come to visit you. (12)

In a surprising twist, the end of the poem asks "Who may this singer be," and reveals that it is the speaker himself: "Know you by this, the lover's chant,/ 'Tis I that am your visitant" (12).

The language of this poem is deliberately archaic, and the scene is metaphorical rather than realistic, evocative of Romeo and Juliet only in its images of evening and night falling, of music and wooing. But in the next poem the figure of a Juliet becomes more explicit, and the mood lightens as the lover appears to hear her singing happily in response:

> Lean out of the window,
> Goldenhair,
> I heard you singing
> A merry air. (13)

The lover is no longer at her gate wooing her, but in a room, reading, with the fireplace fire dancing its images on the floor, who puts his book aside to hear the merry voice singing in the evening gloom outdoors. If we wished to connect these poems to Joyce's later fictions, we might recall a scene in Joyce's story "The Dead," in which Gabriel Conroy looks at his wife listening to a singer as she stands on a stair, and she later tells him about a delicate tubercular boy who used to sing, and who once stood under her window in the rain out of love for her. The poems derive their unusual tone from an intriguing intersection between the formality of the speaker whose voice projects an adult wisdom, but whose controlled diction cannot suppress the youthful and vibrant emotions it expresses.

As they progress, the moods of the poems of "Chamber Music" become much darker. The sounds of the penultimate poem XXXV are no longer musical and no longer reflect the joy of the beginning:

> All day I hear the noise of waters
> Making moan,
> Sad as the sea-bird is, when going
> Forth alone,
> He hears the winds cry to the waters'
> Monotone. (43)

The allusions to the sound of water predict the importance of rivers and the sea in Joyce's later work. Stephen Dedalus, the young protagonist of *A Portrait of the Artist as a Young Man*, has a magical moment when he sees a young woman wading in a stream by the strand. He is captivated by her loveliness and, as he watches her stirring the water with her foot, the sound arrests him. "The first faint noise of gently moving water broke the silence, low and faint and whispering, faint as the bells of sleep; hither and thither, hither and thither" (*Portrait* 171). Many years later the sound of water still haunts Joyce's writing, and one of the signature chapters of *Finnegans Wake* offers an image of two washerwomen doing laundry in the river Liffey, that is also identified with a female figure named "Anna Livia Plurabelle." Joyce told friends that he wanted to evoke the sounds and rhythms of water in the words of that chapter, and on the night he finished it, he went to listen to the sounds of the river Seine in Paris, to make sure he captured it. He is said to have returned reassured that he did so.

But sound and music are not the only attributes of nature presented in the poems of "Chamber Music," where light and color also play important roles. In the eighth poem a wooded area is described as illuminated by sunlight, "The ways of all the woodland/ Gleam with a soft and golden fire" (16). And light and color also illuminate evening scenes, as in the second poem, which begins with the lines "The twilight turns from amethyst/ To deep and deeper blue" (10). Remembering the evocative quality of such scenes in Joyce's early poems helps us to anticipate the lyricism of his scenes of nature in *Ulysses* and *Finnegans Wake* many years later.

Joyce's poems were not all lyrical, however. Although William Butler Yeats had been surprisingly kind to him, Joyce included him as a target in a satirical poem he wrote in 1904 called "The Holy Office," that attacked some of the prominent Irish literary figures in his day. The complaint in the poem is that while these writers focus on producing aesthetic language and spiritual forays they are ignoring the realities of Irish life, which are left to a realist like Joyce to produce:

> But all these men of whom I speak
> Make me the sewer of their clique.
> That they may dream their dreamy dreams
> I carry off their filthy streams. (*Critical Writings* 151)

His criticism of the Irish literary scene began even earlier. In a 1901 protest, Joyce accused the Irish Literary Theatre of abandoning its original plan to present some of the European plays that were revolutionizing drama in Scandinavia, Germany, and Russia in preference to staging more popular works to please a general public, or "the rabblement," as he called it. In "The Day of the Rabblement"

Joyce argues that a "nation which never advanced so far as a miracle-play affords no literary model to the artist, and he must look abroad," presumably to such Continental writers as "Ibsen, Tolstoy or Hauptmann" who were neglected by the Irish Literary Theatre (*Critical Writings* 70). Other early essays do praise Irish writers, however, including a 1902 piece on James Clarence Mangan. And one of Joyce's most poignant essays, published in 1909, offers a highly sympathetic account of the rise and fall of Oscar Wilde. In "Oscar Wilde: The Poet of 'Salomé'," Joyce describes how Wilde, an Irish writer living in England, fashioned himself as an "Apostle of Beauty," promoted aesthetic ideals in art, and became a "standard of elegance" in the metropolis of London. His success in becoming a celebrity is given some criticism: "In the tradition of the Irish writers of comedy that runs from the days of Sheridan and Goldsmith to Bernard Shaw, Wilde became, like them, court jester to the English" (*Critical Writings* 202). However, Joyce describes the persecution of Wilde that followed his conviction on charges of homosexuality as cruel. "His fall was greeted by a howl of puritanical joy. At the news of his condemnation, the crowd gathered outside the courtroom began to dance a pavane in the muddy street" (*Critical Writings* 203). The essay, written when Joyce lived in Trieste, displays a progressive political affinity coupled with critical skill in analyzing the ongoing vulnerability of Irish artists obliged to operate within a British framework. It thereby offers some insight into Joyce's own decision to emigrate to the Continent rather than to England when he decided to leave Ireland in 1904.

Joyce's later work, the curious 1914 prose poem *Giacamo Joyce*, generally receives little discussion because it was intended less as a literary production than a highly personal and intimate rumination on feelings inspired by an infatuation Joyce developed for one of his students in Trieste. But his 1918 drama *Exiles* is surprisingly intricate with a plot that entails the convoluted connections between four characters, and offers an echo of a biographical move in Joyce's life. The play represents the relationship between two men and two women who have been friends for many years, and who become romantically entangled after one couple's return from a sojourn in Rome, Italy. Joyce and his family had ventured from Trieste to live in Rome in 1906, where he took a job as a bank clerk. It was not a happy experience for him, but instead of returning to Ireland, like the figures in *Exiles*, Joyce took his wife and son back to Trieste after some months. Richard Rowan and his common-law wife and son lived in Rome for a number of years, and their little boy Archie still speaks a bit of Italian. While living in Rome, where Bertha was unhappy, Richard corresponded with a childhood friend named Beatrice Justice and developed some feelings for her. Beatrice has a long time relationship with a childhood friend named Robert Hand, to whom she was engaged for a time, and Robert, in turn, has begun to make advances to Bertha, Richard's spouse. The play takes place over the course of two days, and presents a number of intense conversations between the men and women over their assorted relationships. The challenge Joyce meets in this play is to keep all the relationships uncertain and ambivalent, caring and loving, resenting and coming close to hating, trusting and distrusting, all voiced in dialogue. In the first conversation, Richard asks Beatrice "Do you think I have acted towards you—badly?" in reference to a recent conversation they held, and she answers that she asked herself that question but cannot answer it (*Exiles* 5). Richard tells her "You cannot give yourself freely and wholly" (8) and she agrees, with both of them suffering rather than gratified by the conversation. Richard's wife Bertha's own relationship with their friend Robert is more intimate and entails kisses, which Bertha then reports to her husband. "He kissed me." "Long kisses?" Richard asks, and she answers "Yes, the last time" (27). Bertha appears to be indulging in a double betrayal here of both men, which is further complicated when Richard tells Robert that Bertha has told him all that goes on between them. If this play prefigures the adultery theme in *Ulysses*, it also allows us to see how Joyce managed to smooth it out in his later work, maintaining both a level of complexity in the relationship between Leopold Bloom, his wife Molly, and her lover Hugh Boylan, but with a far clearer establishment of causes and motivations and their potential resolutions.

During the years when these early works were written, Joyce was also working on the short stories that would be collected as *Dubliners,* and on his first novel, *A Portrait of the Artist as a Young Man.* The world of literary art experienced a revolution during this period which we now characterize as literary Modernism or modernist art. Such theorists as Charles Darwin, Friedrich Nietzsche, Karl Marx, and Sigmund Freud were revolutionizing thinking about the human condition and the human mind during the late 19th and early 20th century. Joyce demonstrated this impact even in small moments in his fiction, as when he has the young medical student Malachi ("Buck") Mulligan quote Nietzsche's "Thus spake Zarathustra" (*Ulysses* 19) in the first chapter of *Ulysses*, set in 1904.

Literature's response to these influences was to reinvent itself, to make itself "new," as the poet Ezra Pound put it. It did so by giving itself the freedom to experiment with style and language, while nonetheless anchoring itself to what the critic T.E. Hulme termed "Classicism," a return not only to classical themes but also to a formal restraint in writing, using concrete images and a deliberate economy in crafting poetic language. Joyce's own tribute to classicism is seen in the surname of his protagonist Stephen Dedalus, derived from the Greek myth of an artisan living on the island of Crete, who makes wings out of feathers and wax to allow him and his son to fly across the ocean. And Joyce not only derived the title of *Ulysses* from Greek mythology, but gave every episode in the novel a correspondence to characters, places, or incidents in Homer's epic *Odyssey*. T. S. Eliot's 1919 essay "Tradition and the Individual Talent" made another point illustrated in Joyce's use of classicism, namely evidence of the poet's "impersonal" stance in his writing, a strategy best implemented by narration in different voices and not in the single voice of the poet. In *Ulysses,* the episodes are sometimes narrated in the third person, sometimes in the first person, by male voices and female voices, even by such unusual maneuvers as having a voice express how a character might wish to speak if she could, in the language of romance novels, say, rather than how she would actually speak. Joyce's era committed itself to having modernist literature aspire not only to the "new," but also to preserving the historical timelessness found in classical art and literature. This simultaneous grounding in tradition and disciplined writing combined with an impulse toward pushing avant-garde experimentalism to often wild extremes makes Joyce's literary canon so extraordinary. From the solemn poems of "Chamber Music" to the colorful verbal deconstructions of *Finnegans Wake*, Joyce's work encompasses a virtually unprecedented literary universe.

Margot Norris
Irvine, California

1

Introduction: Life and Career

The previous discussion of Joyce's lesser known works alluded to various moments in his life and career, serving as a prelude to a more systematic and detailed biographical portrait of Joyce over the course of his life. Joyce was born in Dublin, Ireland on February 2, 1882, the oldest child of a Catholic family that was initially well off, but whose fortunes declined as each of its 10 children was born and their father, a heavy drinker, failed to find steady work. Joyce was initially sent to a prestigious Jesuit boarding school in County Kildare, where he received the beginning of an excellent education that continued through his college years. Critic Lee Spinks writes that it was at Clongowes Wood College that Joyce "gained his first grounding in Latin, theology and the classics" (*James Joyce: A Critical Guide* 3). But the six-year-old Joyce was also bullied by classmates and unjustly punished over an incident involving his broken glasses—an event that points to the ongoing eye problems he would endure throughout his life.

After his one year at Clongowes, Joyce's father could no longer afford the tuition, but fortunately, the former rector of the boarding school helped Joyce get admitted to the Jesuit high school of Belvedere College in Dublin, which he attended for the next six years. He did well at Belvedere, acting in a play and winning prizes for academic achievement. His adolescence led him to an encounter with a prostitute that created a religious crisis for him, an experience echoed in detail in the retreat episode in *Portrait*. Like Stephen Dedalus, Joyce too was approached by one of his mentors to consider joining the priesthood, and he too declined. During his early years, religion and politics also came into critical conflict in Ireland, creating a painful moment in Joyce's young life that too becomes a reference in *Portrait.* The Protestant politician Charles Stewart Parnell, a champion of Irish independence from Britain, was denounced by the Catholic Church after his affair with a married woman was disclosed. This created conflict not only in Ireland at large, but also within families, as Joyce portrayed in the devastating Christmas feud in the novel.

At 16, Joyce continued his education at University College, Dublin. There he expanded his intellectual grounding in the art and culture of his day, to extend beyond England and Ireland to the Continental literature that had revolutionized fiction writing in the late 19th and early 20th centuries. This included the works of Henrik Ibsen, and later also the writings of Gustave Flaubert, Gerhart Hauptmann, and Leo Tolstoy, among others, inspiring Joyce to write "The Day of the Rabblement." In 1900, he wrote a play titled *A Brilliant Career*, which was inspired by Ibsen's work, but unfortunately did not survive. He also began writing poetry. Joyce scholar and biographer Morris Beja reports that in 1902 the distinguished Irish poet W. B. Yeats responded to some of the poems by telling Joyce "your technique in verse is very much better than the technique of any young Dublin man I have met during my time" (*James Joyce: A Literary Life* 27). Another of his writing experiments took a form that might be considered "prose poems," as biographer Richard Ellmann calls them, brief works that have become known as his 'epiphanies' (*James Joyce* 83). Ellmann points out that their aim was to reveal "the whatness of a thing," and thereby to make "the soul of the commonest object . . . radiant." After college, Joyce decided to study medicine in Paris (he was by then fluent in French, German, and Italian), and Yeats kindly met with him on his stopover in London before he continued his journey abroad. His Paris sojourn of eighteen months was not successful. Joyce stayed there until April of 1903 when a telegram from his family informed him that his mother was dying, forcing him to hurry back home. She died several months later, and Joyce's refusal to pray at her deathbed—he had distanced himself from the Catholic Church by that time—inspired a similar event for his character Stephen Dedalus in his 1922 *Ulysses*.

After his mother's death, Joyce was somewhat aimless and unclear about how to proceed with his life. He took a teaching job for a few weeks, and since he had a beautiful tenor voice, entered a singing contest. He continued experimenting with some writing, jotting moments of his life that would later emerge in *Stephen Hero* and *Portrait*. Then in the summer and fall of 1904, three momentous events changed the course of his entire life. In June, Joyce met a young woman from western Ireland named Nora Barnacle, who was working as a chambermaid at Finn's Hotel in Dublin. Morris Beja writes "She was a self-confident woman, with a sharp wit, and striking in appearance, with beautiful auburn hair" (23), and Lee Spinks agrees, calling her "spirited, independent, and self-contained" with a "direct and unaffected manner" (22-23). Joyce's attempt to get a date with her didn't work immediately, but on June 16, 1904, they went walking together, leading to a life-long relationship. To celebrate this meeting, Joyce set *Ulysses* on that very day.

Another real-life event is also commemorated in *Ulysses*. In September of that year, Joyce shared a room with a friend named Oliver St John Gogarty. They lived in the Martello tower, a military tower available for rental at Sandycove, along the south coast of Dublin. Joyce was there for only five days, but his tense relationship with Gogarty and a British visitor named Samuel Chenevix Trench is represented in the opening chapter of *Ulysses* in a series of strained conversations between Stephen Dedalus and two young men at the Martello tower. Soon after this experience, Joyce decided to leave Ireland for the Continent, but this time not alone. Although he did not want to marry, he asked Nora Barnacle to elope with him, and in early October they left for London and Paris by boat. And so Joyce's new life on the Continent began.

Joyce's plan had been to teach English at a Berlitz school in Zurich, but it turned out that no positions were available. He ended up teaching in Italy instead, first in the city of Pola and then in Trieste, where he and Nora lived for 10 years until the outbreak of World War I. Less than a year after leaving Ireland, Nora gave birth to a baby boy they named Giorgio. Before too long Joyce invited his brother Stanislaus to join his family in Trieste. Joyce now began serious work on the short stories that would eventually be published as '*Dubliners*', but an early attempt to get them published in Ireland failed, much to his disappointment. In 1906, he took a job in Rome and took his family there, hoping for a better life. But it turned out not to be a good venue for him, and the Joyces returned to Trieste. This experience inspired some of the characters in his play *Exiles*, which he wrote some years later and published in 1918.

In 1907, Nora gave birth to a little girl they named Lucia, and in the same year, the poem collection of *Chamber Music* was published. Joyce also began publishing a series of articles in the Trieste newspaper *Il Piccolo della Sera*, most focused on Ireland and Irish art. In 1909, Joyce made his first trip back to Ireland so his father could meet his grandson, Giorgio. On his return trip back to Trieste, he brought his younger sister Eva with him. Still in her teens, Eva loved the movie theaters in Trieste and complained to her brother about the lack of similar venues in Dublin. This spurred Joyce to find some entrepreneurs who were willing to invest in a cinema in Dublin. Joyce traveled there to get the project—called the Volta Theatre—started, and this time returned to Trieste with another sister, Eileen. But the Volta did not get off the ground well, and Joyce returned to teaching.

During the last several years Joyce had been writing short stories and continued working on a novel of sorts that he initially titled *Stephen Hero*. He hoped to publish his short stories as a collection to be called *Dubliners*, and on another trip to Ireland he tried to negotiate its publication, but ran into some difficulties. While all this was in progress, Joyce developed some friendships that were to play important roles in his developing career. One such relationship was with a middle-aged student he tutored, a businessman named Ettore Schmitz, who later became a famous writer under the pseudonym of Italo Svevo. He was Jewish, one of a number of Jewish acquaintances Joyce befriended in Trieste, and this experience may have later influenced his decision to make the protagonist of *Ulysses* a Jew ("more or less," as Beja describes him [57]). Another Jewish student named Amalia Popper inspired Joyce's "notebook" (as his biographer Richard Ellmann calls it [342]). Titled *Giacomo Joyce*, its strange descriptions are generally construed as expressing an infatuation Joyce may have had with the young woman.

The years before and after 1914 were a turning point in Joyce's career and his life. In 1913 he heard from an American named Ezra Pound, who had learned about Joyce's skill in writing from Yeats, and who asked Joyce if he would send him some of his work for possible publication in a new journal called *The Egoist*. Pound, who eventually became a distinguished poet in his own right, offered Joyce critical professional support in the ensuing years. Joyce sent Pound not only his short stories but also a sample from his novel which he now titled *A Portrait of the Artist as a Young Man*, and by 1914 *The Egoist* began serial publication of the book. One of the editors of the journal, a woman named Harriet Shaw Weaver, became a major financial supporter not only of Joyce's work, but also of his family, for years to come.

By 1915, all of *Portrait* had appeared in serial form and was published as a book the following year. Joyce's career was launched. However, the outbreak of World War I created a major turmoil in Joyce's life. In spite of its largely Italian population, Trieste belonged to the Austro-Hungarian Empire up to that time, which made the political situation for technically British citizens like the Joyce family complicated and risky when war with Italy broke out. As a result, they moved to Zurich in neutral Switzerland, where they lived until the end of the war. By then Joyce had begun working on the new novel that would become *Ulysses*, while still teaching private pupils. Joyce also became involved in a theater company called "The English Players," which unfortunately involved him in a complicated dispute with an actor who complained about insufficient pay, a conflict that resulted in legal actions. But plays continued to be produced during this time, and Nora and the children actually took part in one of the productions. Joyce also made a number of new friends in Zurich, including a man named Frank Budgen with whom he remained on friendly terms for many years. Also around that time Joyce, who had begun having eye problems as early as 1908, suffered a serious attack of glaucoma that required surgery. As with *Portrait*, initial publication of chapters of *Ulysses* began in a journal, an American production called *The Little Review*, where the new book's objectionable language and concepts created censorship problems. The editors, Jane Heap and Margaret Anderson, were eventually tried in a U.S. court for the work's supposed obscenity, and were both fined and forbidden to continue publication.

The Joyce family left Zurich and returned to Trieste the year after World War I ended, in 1919. But they found the city much changed, and a year later, at the urging of Ezra Pound, whom Joyce had finally met in person, they moved to Paris; they lived there until the outbreak of World War II. Thanks to the support of Harriet Shaw Weaver and another patron, Joyce was able to devote himself to his writing, and after having worked on *Ulysses* for seven years, Joyce finished the work in 1921. The search for a publisher began, made complicated by the fact that its reputation for obscenity deterred English or American publishers from considering it. Fortunately, a year earlier Joyce had met an American woman who ran a bookstore called "Shakespeare and Company," which became an important institution for English-speaking expatriates living in Paris at that time. Her name was Sylvia Beach and she and Joyce became good friends. When Joyce told her of his worry that his book might never be published, their discussion led to a decision to have "Shakespeare and Company" publish it for him. It was unusual to have a bookstore owner with no publishing experience undertake such a project, but Beach found an excellent printer named Maurice Darantière who worked in Dijon. The publication process was arduous, with Joyce making many changes to the proofs, but the first copies of *Ulysses*, with blue covers reflecting the Greek flag, were finally printed at the beginning of February 1922. In what has become a famous story, we are told that Darantière put two copies of the book on the express train to Dijon on the morning of Joyce's fortieth birthday, February 2, 1922, and instructed the conductor to give them to Sylvia Beach, who was waiting for the train in Paris. She took them and jumped into a taxi, and gave Joyce his first copy of *Ulysses* that morning (Ellmann 524).

The book created a sensation of sorts, and before long copies were being smuggled into the United States where it was not available for legal publication until after a landmark U.S. court decision in 1933. The book's problematic legal status created a crisis of sorts in 1926 when an American publisher named Samuel Roth began to publish an edited serial version of the work, without Joyce's permission, in a journal he ran. Without legal recourse, Joyce turned to the international community to ask authors and others to sign a protest letter, and Morris Beja reports that the signatories included such famous names as Albert Einstein, Ernest Hemingway, Thomas Mann, D.H. Lawrence, and Virginia Woolf, among others (94). The protest had little effect, but the fame of *Ulysses* continued to grow. Beja notes that by the end of the 1920s, Joyce—"certainly not the most widely read of authors in the English language—was probably the most famous" (96). A year after the publication of *Ulysses*, Joyce began working on a new project whose title did not become known until many years later, but which we now know as *Finnegans Wake*.

The period during which Joyce worked on *Finnegans Wake*, 1923 to 1939, was a time of growing success and fame, but also of difficulty and familial tragedy. Writers began to write memoirs and studies of Joyce's work, with Herbert Gorman's *James Joyce: His First Forty Years* appearing in 1924 and Frank Budgen's *James Joyce and the Making of 'Ulysses'* in 1934. The support of Harriet Shaw Weaver allowed the Joyce family to live very comfortably, eating out most evenings at fine restaurants and enjoying pleasant vacations at handsome hotels. New friendships were forged, including one with the young writer, Samuel Beckett. The children seemed to be doing well for a time, given their relocation to three different countries during their youth, which required them to learn Italian, German, and French, even as the family spoke English and Italian at home.

The writing of *Finnegans Wake* posed an immense challenge to Joyce because the work, initially titled *Work in Progress*, was highly experimental, both in its content with an array of characters with constantly fluctuating identities and events—and its style, which included words constantly inflected from English by multiple meanings and by other languages. Critic John Bishop reports that

Joyce claimed he wanted "to write this book about the night" (*Joyce's Book of the Dark* 4), and critic Vincent Cheng takes this notion even further in discussing the *Wake* as "the construct of a dream, the perfect vehicle for repeated motifs and variations, for everything happening at once, for all possibilities and all history in the course of a night's dream" (*Shakespeare and Joyce* 19). Unfortunately, early responses to this new work were more discouraging than encouraging. Ezra Pound, his enthusiastic early supporter, was not impressed, and told Joyce in a letter that "Nothing so far as I can make out, nothing short of divine vision or a new cure for the clapp can possibly be worth all the circumambient peripherization" (Spinks 39). In 1929, hoping to attract attention to his ambitious new work and give it some elucidation, Joyce enlisted the help of a dozen friends and colleagues to write a series of essays on *Work in Progress*, which were published under the Wakean title *Our Exagmination Round His Factification for Incamination of Work in Progress*. The book included essays by Samuel Beckett, William Carlos Williams, and Frank Budgen, among others.

The work on the *Wake* was compounded by other difficulties. Joyce continued to have severe eye problems that required frequent surgeries that diminished his eyesight. His children's lives moved on, with Giorgio marrying in 1930, an event that Morris Beja suggests may have prompted Joyce and Nora to decide to marry in order to legitimize their children's right to any inheritances; they subsequently wed in England in 1931. A year later, Giorgio's wife Helen gave birth to Joyce's grandson who was given the name Stephen, harking back to Joyce's early figure of the artist in his work. Joyce was so touched by his grandson's birth, following the recent death of his father, that he wrote the poem "Ecce Puer" to commemorate it. At around the same time, his daughter Lucia began exhibiting erratic behavior that was eventually diagnosed as schizophrenia, requiring periods of institutionalization, much to Joyce's worry and grief. Lucia had hoped to become a dancer and appeared in a number of recitals in Paris in the later 1920s, and had also taken up drawing. But none of these enterprises proved to hold long-range promise for her. Nor was she successful in finding a partner, and her hope that her father's friend, Samuel Beckett, might take a romantic interest in her also led to disappointment. Morris Beja reports that on February 2, 1932, the day of "Joyce's fiftieth birthday, she became violent and threw a chair at Nora" (114). One of the family's efforts to help Lucia took them to Switzerland in 1934, to seek the professional advice of the psychiatrist Carl Jung. But neither visits to psychiatric doctors nor stays with Joyce's friends, including

Harriet Shaw Weaver, helped her condition in any productive way. In March of 1936, Lucia was finally admitted to a mental institution in Ivry in France. Critic Carol Loeb Shloss offers a complex account of the painful events leading up to this institutionalization (*Lucia Joyce* 376–380), and notes that a weekly visitor to Lucia during her stay there was Samuel Beckett. Giorgio's wife Helen also suffered a serious nervous breakdown in 1939 which ended their marriage, and Helen moved back to the United States.

Although these assorted problems caused Joyce to interrupt work on *Finnegans Wake,* he finally came to the end and finished it late in 1938. Every effort was made to have it published on his February 2 birthday, and although it was still in page proofs and not actually in print until a few months later, Joyce did indeed receive the first copy of *Finnegans Wake* on his 57th birthday in 1939. Morris Beja refers to the book as "one of the most amazing and formidable works in all of literary history" (121).

By this time Europe was in turmoil with the approach of World War II. Joyce was keenly aware of the situation and "gave concrete assistance to a number of Jews attempting to flee from German control," according to Beja (122). The Joyce family began to worry about remaining in Paris with the threat of an invasion by German forces, and in December 1939 they moved to a French village where their friend Maria Jolas had a home. They stayed there until near the end of 1940 when they once again moved to Zurich, Switzerland, where they had spent the years of World War I. Joyce, who had been suffering from severe stomach pains for some time felt his condition become more extreme in Zurich. This was not surprising, given his anxiety for the safety of his daughter Lucia, who had been moved to another hospital but remained institutionalized in France. Early in January, Joyce suffered such severe pain that he was taken to a Zurich hospital where his condition was diagnosed as a perforated ulcer. Surgery was performed, but on January 13, 1941, just weeks shy of his 58th birthday, James Joyce died. He was buried in a Zurich cemetery. All other members of Joyce's family survived the war, and his wife Nora was eventually buried next to him.

Joyce's death ended an extraordinary literary career, whose output will be examined in careful detail in the following chapters, with detailed descriptions and discussion of the stories of *Dubliners*, his early novel *A Portrait of the Artist as a Young Man,* the landmark *Ulysses,* and his last work, *Finnegans Wake.*

2

Dubliners

Ulysses would not be Joyce's first work to run into censorship problems. *Dubliners* was published in 1914 after a long and difficult effort: editors and printers objected to references in the text and demanded alterations often not amenable to Joyce. Later Joyce claimed that over a period of nine years, 40 publishers had rejected this work.

The volume consists of 15 stories set in Dublin at the turn of the 20th century, each representing the relatively ordinary lives of its residents. Their stories are told in a chronological sequence from the experiences of childhood, to those of adolescence, followed by adulthood and maturity. In a number of letters, Joyce made it clear that he intended the collection to offer "a moral history of my country." He set it in Dublin, which seemed to him "the centre of paralysis." One device for having the stories achieve this goal was to imbue them with those moments Joyce called "epiphany," the sudden insight or understanding of something significant revealed in an ordinary event, encounter, or experience. Some of the stories are grounded in Joyce's own biographical experience. The story "An Encounter," for example, is based on his memory of playing hooky with his brother Stanislaus and running into a strange man in a meadow. Many of Dublin's actual locations are either mentioned or can be inferred from the narrative, including the house that is the setting for "The Dead," the last story in the collection; the 15 Usher's Island address is now a Dublin landmark. These features of both factual and thematic content in the stories are complemented by complications in the way many of the stories are told.

The first three stories of childhood appear to be told in a kind of double narration, a first person account that may be either a child speaking of his experiences or an adult recounting childhood events. In addition, many of the stories appear to have gaps or mysteries embedded in them. We are given events, but it is not always entirely clear what happened and often difficult to determine what they mean. In "Two Gallants" for example, a man goes on a date with a young servant woman, and afterward, she runs into the home where she works and comes out with a gold coin that she gives him. We are not told where she gets the money, why she gives it to him, or why he might have asked her for it. This element of ambiguity and mystery makes the stories intriguing, but requires the reader to reconstruct the scenarios and speculate about what is going on and what an occurrence might mean. Therefore, the "epiphany" or moment of insight is the reader's rather than a character's, and is often required to be earned by interpretation rather than offered by the narration.

I will now turn to each of the 15 stories in sequence and examine them from these various perspectives to explore not only their content but also their mode of telling.

"The Sisters"

The title of this story is puzzling because the sisters appear only in the last part, where they offer little more than a background for events whose foreground is held by a young boy and a priest. The story opens with a first-person narrator speaking *in media res*—that is, beginning in the middle—telling us "There was no hope for him this time: it was the third stroke" (*Dubliners,* 3). A few details suggest that the speaker is a boy concerned about a man who is dying: "He had often said to me: *I am not long for this world.*" The boy passes the man's house every night for signs of a change, and says that "as I gazed up at the window I said softly to myself the word *paralysis.*" Paralysis is a common symptom of a stroke, but also a metaphor for the inability to act that Joyce appeared to attribute to Dublin's moral stagnation as a city that "seemed to me the centre of paralysis." The boy comes down to supper one evening to hear a conversation between a visitor named Cotter and the aunt and uncle whose home he shares. It now becomes clear that the dying man was a priest and the boy's friend, and that he has indeed died. The boy appears not to like Cotter, and Cotter's conversation is troublesome because it hints that there was something "queer" about Father Flynn that should make one wary of allowing him a friendship with a boy. "Tiresome old fool!" the boy thinks in response to this conversation, but as he drifts off to sleep, he imagines the priest's face murmuring as if "it desired to confess something," making his soul feel it is "receding into some pleasant and vicious region" (5). These various innuendoes suggest that the priest may have molested the boy in some way, but the boy's thoughts never represent or concede such an assumption, and the reader, therefore, confronts a dilemma of moral judgment, trying to determine how to feel about the relationship as the narration represents it. The next day, the boy passes Father Flynn's house and confirms that he has indeed died. He now revisits their relationship in his mind, the last days when the priest's hands trembled so much that he spilled the loose snuff tobacco the boy had brought him, and the earlier days when the erudite man posed difficult questions that showed the boy "how complex and mysterious were certain institutions of the church which I had always regarded as the simplest acts" (6). This information adds to the complexity of the relationship which clearly served to inspire the boy with the confidence that allowed him to judge old Cotter as an imbecile. That evening the aunt takes the boy to Father Flynn's house where his sisters Eliza and Nannie are holding a vigil by their brother's coffin, and where Eliza describes his life as overburdened and "crossed" (10). She concludes with an incident of a fellow priest finding Father Flynn alone in the confessional of an empty chapel "laughing-like softly to himself" (11). The brief story has certainly conveyed a depth of feeling and caring by the boy and the sisters about a man whose troubled nature may have pushed against, or over, the edge of "moral stagnation," as Joyce called it.

"An Encounter"

If the possibility of perverse behavior is left ambiguous and indefinite in "The Sisters," the next story, "An Encounter," makes it perfectly explicit. Two boys decide to skip school to play hooky, to go on a "day's miching," as Joyce's brother Stanislaus described the biographical experience behind the story. At the end of their journey, they encounter a strange old man who engages one of them in a troublesome conversation about juvenile punishment. However, the story's beginning offers no early clues or indications of how the boys' adventure is going to unfold or how it is going to end. As a result, the ending produces a shock not only to the boys in the story but also to the reader as well.

This draws our attention to the fact that "An Encounter" opens with the subject of reading about adventure and the adventure of reading. "It was Joe Dillon who introduced the wild west to us. He had a little library made up of old numbers of *The Union Jack, Pluck* and *The Halfpenny Marvel*" (11). The boys are introduced not to the Wild West per se, but to popular literary representations in pieces like *The*

Apache Chief that, in turn, inspire the boys to imitate what they read by fighting pitched "Indian battles" on the grass in their back gardens. But the boy narrator soon tires of what he terms this "mimic warfare" and decides that "I wanted real adventures to happen to myself" (13). And so he and a friend skip a day of school and head out to find some adventure without any sense of what that might be.

At first, it turns out to be a game with young Mahony playing an Indian by chasing some girls and mock fighting with their little friends. They do see barges and sailing vessels and cross the river on a ferry, and the narrator mysteriously hopes to find sailors with green eyes, although he refuses to explain why—"I had some confused notion ...." (16). This ellipsis obliges the reader to speculate on the meaning of this gap, and to consider such possibilities as that "green" may have referred to homosexuality in Joyce's day. This occurs to the reader only in retrospect, after the boys encounter a man termed a "queer old josser," and the narrator notices with surprise that the man has "bottlegreen eyes" (19). The man does not touch the boys physically; his molestation is verbal only and channeled through literature by first engaging with them about reading. "He asked us whether we had read the poetry of Thomas Moore or the works of Sir Walter Scott and Lord Lytton" (17). He then slyly turns the conversation to girls, and after Mahony takes off, to the subject of whipping. "He said that my friend was a very rough boy and asked did he get whipped often at school" (19). With this the monologue turns into a verbal expression of a sadistic bent, and the boy waits for a pause in the speech to make a getaway. "I went up the slope calmly but my heart was beating quickly with fear that he would seize me by the ankles" (19-20). The boys' adventure has been a transition from children's penny novels into pornography, and as critic R. B. Kershner points out, the boy has come to realize that fictions are "part of complex, embedded ideologies whose ramifications may be baffling or dangerous" (*Joyce, Bakhtin, and Popular Literature,* 46).

"Araby"

The beginning of the third story, "Araby," appears to hark back to "The Sisters" for just a moment, conjuring up a house on North Richmond Street that had belonged to a priest before his death. The boy knows the priest only from a few things left behind, including some books and a rusty bicycle pump. But his narrative soon makes the quiet house in the quiet neighborhood come to life with the play of children, the odor of stables and music from the harness of horses, and the glow of streetlights. The name of one of his playmates conjures that of the 19th-century Irish poet James Clarence Mangan, and in retrospect, we will find in the name the promise of romance under the glow of the Middle East that had also entranced the poet, as Joyce noted in a 1902 essay.

It is Mangan's sister, who is never given a first name, who inspires what we would now call a "crush" in the boy narrator, and who tells him about a bazaar she cannot attend called "Araby." The story is, therefore, a sad one, the tale of a young romantic whose descriptions of the life around him are intensely poetic and who is filled with sensitivity and longings for love and romance. But the boy will be defeated by the realities of ordinary life that bring him back down to an earth where uncles are drunken and forgetful, and where bazaars are places of money, commerce, and workers rather than of oriental splendor.

There is little ambiguity about the boy's feelings for Mangan's sister. He watches her from under the blind of a parlor window and then follows her on the way to school, passing her so that she will notice that he has been behind her. One rainy night he goes into the drawing-room where the priest has died and pressing his trembling hands together, he murmurs "*O love! O love!* many times" (22). The reader can infer that the girl is not oblivious to the boy's infatuation and that this is why she shares with him her disappointment at being obliged to miss Araby, which she assumes will be "a splendid bazaar." He offers to mitigate her sadness by bringing her something from the bazaar, and we are now given the effects of his anticipation and planning for this event, which distracts him at school and casts "an eastern enchantment" over him (23). His Orientalism is inflected with the exotic and the aesthetic, and although he never hears the poem by Caroline Norton called *The Arab's Farewell to his Steed*, which his uncle starts to recite to his aunt, we can imagine that its theme of nobility would have resonated with the boy.

But on the evening of the bazaar, everything goes awry. His uncle is out drinking and returns home so late that the boy arrives at the site when it is effectively preparing to close. All that appears to remain is "the magical name" (25) of *Araby* on the building, and when he hears the trite flirtation of the shop girl with two fellows, he cannot even bring himself to buy a promised gift for Mangan's sister. The failure of romance to materialize in the reality of his daily life leaves him completely crushed. "Gazing up into the darkness I saw myself as a creature driven and derided by vanity: and my eyes burned with anguish and anger" (26).

"Eveline"

The three stories of childhood all give us boy narrators with something to look up to or forward to: an erudite priest, the prospect of gratifying adventure, the delight of romance and a romantic setting. But in each case, the realities of the flawed adult world intrude to dim the brightness of childhood vision.

"Eveline" now presents the first story of adolescence. At its center there is ambiguity: does its heroine, Eveline Hill, try to preserve childhood hopes and dreams, or has the dreariness of adult life already defeated her before she has even settled in it. The story offers only two scenes. The first shows Eveline sitting at her window with two letters on her lap, one to her brother and the other to her father. Unlike the childhood stories, her thoughts are narrated in the third person as she reflects on a childhood and present life made difficult by a taxing father, a situation that has caused her to decide to leave home. She plans to travel to Argentina with Frank, a young man she has begun to like. The second scene shows her at the dock where the two are about to board the ship bound for Buenos Ayres. Tormented by indecision that paralyzes her, Eveline holds back and sees Frank go forward without her. Did she make a wise decision or a foolish one?

The venerable critic Hugh Kenner argued that Eveline was lucky to abort the voyage because Frank in all likelihood was a seducer who would probably have abandoned her ("Molly's Masterstroke"). His reading places the story in the genre of young women deluded by the fantasies generated by romance novels, the kind of situation presented in Gustav Flaubert's *Madame Bovary*, for example. But other critics such as Sidney Feshbach place the story into the larger category of immigration narratives, reminding us that the difficult life in Ireland following the Great Famine of the 1840s prompted thousands of Irish people to leave their country in hopes of a better life elsewhere. Eveline's painful decision may reflect the anxiety of many people in her day, wondering if a tolerable but dreary existence at home was safer than a risky adventure with a totally uncertain outcome abroad. The narration makes this decision unpredictable, incapable of being adjudicated for its wisdom—not only for Eveline—but for the reader as well. As a result, we are left with the sad prospect that the downturns in the boys' lives in the first three stories may not find redemption in adulthood, and instead, encounter further challenges that may or may not be met successfully.

Eveline will hopefully not end her life as pitifully as her demented mother, but the signs of promise are sparse. Her childhood—like that of the boys—had its pleasant moments of outdoor play, and she concedes that her father "was not so bad then" (27), and recently even looked after her when she was not feeling well. In earlier days the family even went on a picnic, with her father "putting on her mother's bonnet to make the children laugh" (30). Yet there is no question that, at age 19, life is difficult for Eveline, with her father's control and threats, and the responsibilities of maintaining an entire household, in addition to a dreary job. The story's realism lies precisely in these ambiguities and complexities with their lack of a clear answer to a best course of action.

"After the Race"

To assure that adolescence and young adulthood are difficult not only for the relatively poor, like Eveline, Joyce endows the protagonist of "After the Race" with all the advantages and promise of a prosperous life. We encounter the 26-year-old Jimmy Doyle in a racing car with an international group of friends, happy with their success at a solid finish—although Jimmy "was too excited to be genuinely happy" (33).

His is clearly a different world from Eveline's. Jimmy has a father wealthy and devoted enough to send him to excellent schools in England, Dublin, and Cambridge, and he has a substantial sum of money under his control even at a relatively early age. This money is a factor in the background of the story, and yet it lies at its heart in a crucial respect. Although the story will describe chiefly a delightful evening spent with a group of scintillating French, Hungarian, English, and American friends—including an "exquisite" dinner and a merry trip to the Kingstown harbor followed by a jovial card game on an American's yacht—we eventually infer that Jimmy's friendships are all about his money. "[H]e was about to stake the greater part of his substance" by investing in his friend Ségouin's "motor business" (34), a project approved by his father and presumably a source of the fellows' interest in honoring Jimmy with inclusion in their professional and social events on this day. With its focus on Jimmy's pleasures and social timidities in relation to his worldly friends, the narration makes a card game by happily inebriated students a source of enjoyment rather than a deliberate gambit to defraud the naïve Irish youth of his investment.

We are never told that this is what the card game was all about and are simply given the wherewithal to infer this, without any clear evidence. But, of course, it makes perfect sense: why should Ségouin take Jimmy's money as an investment when, by making sure that Jimmy loses a fortune in the card game, he can have it free and clear, with perhaps only a share paid to conniving friends. "How much had he written away?" (38) Jimmy wonders, as he watches the last round of the game, before he will lean on the table, his head between his hands, "counting the beats of his temples" (38). We can only imagine the reaction of his father, and the effect of a loss of his entire fortune on his future.

Placed next to Eveline Hill's story, Jimmy Doyle's enlarges the diversity of *Dubliners* by widening the broader scope of social and economic class, without losing sight of the challenges and difficulties that can afflict the city's young people at critical moments in their lives, whatever their situations. The story also complicates a portrayal of Irish oppression by giving it a tangential political component with its focus on the disadvantages produced by inexperience and lack of sophistication in its upwardly mobile classes.

"Two Gallants"

Joyce's thematic pairing of *Dubliners* stories comes into intriguing view in "Two Gallants." Once again, money will be in the background and yet at the center of a story at the same time, and again, this will not be revealed to the reader except through clues that invite us to guess what is going on. "Two Gallants" also focuses on friendship, although the characters of Corley and Lenehan belong to the opposite end of the social and economic spectrum from the world of Jimmy Doyle.

The third person narration begins with a conversation between the two men about women, with Lenehan paying tribute to Corley as a "gay Lothario" (41) or attractive ladies' man in spite of his large, globular, and oily head that sweats in all weathers. But Corley's treatment of women is anything but gallant, judging from his own account of how he quickly stopped spending money on them, and how one of his early lovers ended up on the "turf" as a prostitute. On this particular night, Corley has a date with a young "slavey"—a domestic servant—who apparently likes him enough to bring him cigarettes and cigars, possibly stolen from her master, and pays for the tram on their trips to Donnybrook, where they carry out their assignation. Corley has no intention of rewarding her interest in him with any sort of commitment, and has even kept his real name from her ("She doesn't know my name" [40]) to avoid future complications.

The mystery at the heart of "Two Gallants" is the question of

Lenehan's interest in this relationship. Is it simply a casual and perhaps voyeuristic curiosity about how a fellow manages this sort of affair? That's the impression we are given at the beginning of the story. But after the men spot the young woman, some curious tensions emerge. Lenehan wants a look at her, and arranges to meet Corley at 10 o'clock when he returns from his date. Why? As Corley and the young woman go off, Lenehan's narrated thoughts reveal that he appears to be virtually broke, hungry after having eaten only two biscuits all day, and able to order only a plate of peas and some ginger beer for supper rather than the much tastier-looking ham and plum-pudding in the eatery window. Thinking about Corley on his date brings out a sense of despair in him, making him feel "his own poverty of purse and spirit," along with weariness at still "knocking about" at the age of 31, rather than settling down to a decent life (46).

As he waits to meet Corley, he begins to be both excited and anxious about whether "Corley would pull it off all right" (47). Pull what off? What is going on here? When Corley does return with the young woman, Lenehan follows them to what is presumably the house where she works, watches her enter the house, come back out toward Corley, and disappear inside again. Lenehan follows Corley, and badgers him to tell him "Did it come off?" (48). Corley finally responds by opening his hand and revealing a small gold coin.

The reader is left to speculate what this evening was all about, and our best guess is that Corley owes the broke Lenehan some money and has no means to repay it except to prod the young slavey to steal it from her employer. Destitution dogs these young Dubliners, and the consequences for the young woman will be disastrous if her employers dismiss her for stealing: it would be impossible for her to find another job, and she could end up as a prostitute like one of Corley's earlier women. If the impressionable Jimmy Doyle was the victim in the previous story, the young slavey's victimization in this one is infinitely more cruel.

"The Boarding House"

The next story still features an adolescent—19-year-old Polly Mooney—and also focuses on an exploitation of sorts, although the victim here is not Polly but Bob Doran, a man in his 30s, living in the boarding house run by Polly's mother.

The plot is relatively straightforward: the older Doran has begun a relationship with the young Polly Mooney, an occurrence that her mother observes and uses to force Doran into what we would now call a "shotgun wedding." We can readily infer this from the rather dry and bland narration, even though two scenes are missing: Mrs. Mooney's confrontation with and possible threats to Bob Doran, and the unhappy man's ensuing marriage proposal to Polly. Neither scene is represented, and the story is thereby robbed of its most exciting narrative possibilities. Why would Joyce write it like this when he could have made it so much more dramatic and entertaining? Whenever Joyce builds elisions like this into his stories, he appears to do so in order to present a challenge to the reader, and this challenge is often ethical, forcing the reader to figure out how to arrive at a fair judgment of the rights and wrongs of a complicated social situation.

Many questions spring to mind. Is Polly's father, "a shabby stooped little drunkard" who eventually attacks his wife with a cleaver, also a victim of a shotgun wedding? Is Mrs. Mooney—*The Madam*, as her residents call her—a madam in more ways than one, intent on prostituting her daughter to the first respectable and solvent young man who will then be forced into marrying her? Is Bob Doran wholly the victim of Mrs. Mooney's plot or should he have seen the danger of his little dalliance with Polly, avoiding it rather than risking his reputation and livelihood in the event of, say, a possible pregnancy? He is better educated than the Mooneys, and while he may not have guessed that "he was being had" (54), he clearly had no intention of marrying Polly until confronted with the mother's righteousness and the possible threat of her burly brother's violence. Also, he is not a total innocent, having "sown his wild oats" (54) in his youth, and living a regular life "nine tenths of the year," suggesting some carousing during the remaining weeks. And what about Polly herself? Is she the innocent victim of both parties, a dim and possibly impaired young woman unaware of her mother's manipulation or does she have an inkling of the background ("she did not wish it to be thought that in her wise innocence she had divined the intention behind her mother's tolerance" [52]). Does her little song, "*I am a .... naughty girl*" (51) contain a tiny bit of truth, as *Ulysses* suggests, where rumors are circulated about the now married Polly exposing herself to some men "without a stitch on her" at two in the morning (*Ulysses* 249)? What if Polly's sweetness toward Doran and her ostensible despair with the present situation ("She would put an end to herself, she said" [54]) collude consciously or unconsciously with her mother's plan? The lives of Dubliners are complicated, and so are the moral judgments confronting their readers.

"A Little Cloud"

Although by now we should have moved from adolescence to adulthood, we still get a subtle reversal of roles in this story of a seemingly childish man named Chandler, who is actually more grown-up than his supposedly worldly friend, Gallaher, who still has the impulses and values of a wild teenager. What keeps this perspective from being clear is the narrative point of view, which tells the story of the evening meeting of the two men in the spirit of Chandler's self-deprecating sense of things.

The story begins with Chandler's admiring thoughts about Gallaher, the friend from his youth who had gone to London eight years before and had become "a brilliant figure on the London press" (57). Gallaher has returned to Dublin for the first time since his departure and will meet with his friend for drinks at an elegant place called "Corless." The narrative voice introduces the protagonist as "Little Chandler," as people refer to him, explaining that although he is not particularly short, "he gave one the idea of being a little man" (57) due to a neat appearance and quiet manners. Chandler's own thoughts seem to corroborate this judgment as he laments his dull job as a law clerk and his quiet life, and reveals his love of poetry and a suppressed wish to be a published poet, perhaps of the "Celtic school." He clearly envies the now successful Gallaher, who displays his newfound cosmopolitanism by injecting French phrases into his orders to the waiters at Corless. Gallaher chides his friend for provincialism and lack of travel "Go to London, or Paris: Paris, for choice" (62), while boasting of his own unsavory Continental experiences.

The narration telling us of this encounter consistently refers to the men as Little Chandler and Ignatius Gallaher, keeping our focus on Chandler's diminution in contrast to Gallaher's professional persona. But Chandler's sober judgment begins to see through his friend's patronizing pomposity and, in a surprising challenge, he tries to present marriage and family as a positive metric for adulthood, a position Gallaher rejects by making it clear he plans to use marriage to get rich: "There are hundreds—what am I saying?—thousands of rich Germans and Jews, rotten with money, that'd only be too glad" (67).

Sadly, Chandler goes home to his wife and child without the satisfaction of acknowledging that he is both a better man than Gallaher and has a potentially better life. Instead, his perspective is now clouded with dissatisfaction and disappointment that he tries to remedy with poetry while his wife goes out to buy tea. But as Chandler is reading Byron (not Celtic poetry), his baby begins to cry, and in his frustration, he shouts at him to "Stop!"—causing the child to produce a hysterical fit of screaming that infuriates his wife on her return. The way the story is told produces an ethical dilemma for the reader who is encouraged both by the narration and by Chandler's thoughts to see him as an effeminate weakling rather than as the responsible family man he is in spite of his timidity. The reader thereby risks falling victim to Chandler's own bent for self-deprecation rather than being spurred to stand up for him.

"Counterparts"

We learn little of Thomas Chandler's life as a clerk in his law firm at the King's Inns, but "Counterparts" takes us into the work-day life of Farrington, a copyist in a law firm. Such 19th century short stories as Herman Melville's "Bartleby, the Scrivener" or Nikolai Gogol's "The Overcoat" present the working life of scriveners as dull and uneventful, and while Chandler's may resemble theirs, Farrington's does not. In the first sentence Farrington's boss is described as "furious," and Farrington is subjected to Mr. Alleyne's critical harangues and cruel reprimands all day. Unlike the sober "little" Chandler, Farrington is a large, hulking figure with a face red from drinking, who towers over his boss, "a little man wearing goldrimmed glasses on a clean-shaven face" (70), who repeatedly upbraids him, mimics and humiliates him in front of others, and threatens him with dismissal. The situation comes to a crisis of sorts when Alleyne calls Farrington a "*know-nothing*" in front of a client and co-workers and asks him "Do you think me an utter fool?" Farrington retorts by blurting out that he doesn't think "that's a fair question to put to me" (75). Alleyne is furious at this response and Farrington knows "his life would be a hell to him" at work from now on. We see him try to survive this horrendous day by first sneaking out for a drink, then pawning his watch at the end of a day so he can drown his misery with a night of drinking with friends. He ends up going home to an empty house. His wife is at chapel, the kitchen fire out, and it is left to his little boy to try to cook him some supper. At this moment his frustrations erupt in violence, and he turns into a version of Alleyne, mimicking and terrifying his little boy and beating him with a stick, his behavior making this the most violent story in *Dubliners.*

The reader is once again presented with an ethical dilemma: should Farrington, a victim of his boss's relentless taunting, incite sympathy and pity? Or should Farrington's aggressiveness in beating an innocent child impede such a response? In some respects, this question makes "Counterparts" much more complicated than Melville's or Gogol's stories, and more modern with its implications of the transfers in cycles of abuse that transform victims into becoming abusers themselves. As readers we are obliged to both judge and question our judgment, to feel sympathy and disgust simultaneously for the same individual, while conceding that unless we have endured similar experiences, we should perhaps not feel entitled to judge—all the while knowing that we must.

"Clay"

In "Clay", Joyce once again overturns elements of the preceding story. If "Counterparts" presents an abusive work-place, "Clay" begins by telling us about a woman who works in a laundry where she appears to perform her work beautifully and is consequently respected, appreciated, and lauded by her superiors and co-workers. Telling us that "the cook said you could see yourself in the big copper boilers" (82), the narration suggests that everyone offers Maria high praise. This diverts us from noting that Maria must be the laundry's scullion, and it is not until we ask ourselves some questions about the religious tracts on the walls that we can infer that the place is a charitable rather than an economic institution, possibly a Protestant establishment to support reformed or aging prostitutes, as some critics have suggested.

Maria previously worked for many years as a domestic for a family, and although her station in life is clearly inferior to Farrington's, she appears blessed by the respect, appreciation, and kindness of colleagues and former employers. The narration offers us a flattering portrait of a special evening in Maria's life, when she will visit the family she once worked for to enjoy a Hallowed Eve celebration, stopping on the way there to buy delicacies. When she arrives she enjoys their kind attentions, is offered drinks, plays a game with the children, and ends her evening by performing a moving song at their request. The problem with this construction of the evening in the positive spirit of the narrative voice is that there are numerous incidents that suggest an entirely different interpretation: one that infers that Maria is teased and made fun of by her co-workers, treated with little courtesy by shop-persons, offered no seating on the crowded tram except by an old drunk, and subjected to an embarrassing prank by her friends' children.

When Maria is invited to join in a fortune-telling game that requires her to be blindfolded and select an object on a table, her hand encounters a "soft wet substance" rather than a prayer book or ring to predict her future. The narration never tells us what she touched or what it meant, and the reader is obliged to guess that perhaps it was damp garden dirt, the "clay" in the story's title, that Maria would fear was excrement or some other vile substance. Fortunately, she remains baffled while the offending object is replaced with the prayer book and Maria's only sign that the experience might have rattled her a bit is her skipping a verse of *I dreamt that I dwelt in marble halls*, her farewell song on this evening.

In "Clay" Joyce has compressed two entirely opposing stories—the first of a woman who is loved and respected, and the second of a disdained and humiliated one—into a single piece of writing managed by a narration that the reader is urged to both register and distrust.

"A Painful Case"

If "Clay" is the story of an "old maid," as Maria might have been called in her day, "A Painful Case" tells us about a middle-aged bachelor with a good job as a bank cashier, a very nice room in the suburb of Chapelizod, and an orderly if dull life that appears undisturbed by James Duffy's lack of companions or friends. But once again, Joyce gives us a story with a double, concealed meaning, which will force the reader to uncomfortably try to guess what the tale is really all about.

Duffy's few pleasures include the occasional concert, and at one he befriends a married woman and her grown daughter. Mrs. Sinico's husband and daughter have no objection to her friendship with Duffy. But one night, as their relationship develops and reaches a point of intimacy, Mrs. Sinico takes his hand "passionately" and presses it to her cheek (93). Duffy is shocked and a week later meets Mrs. Sinico in a park to break up with her after a three-hour conversation. As readers, we are more stunned by Duffy's shock and break-up decision than by Mrs. Sinico's loving gesture. We are shocked again when four years later Duffy reads a newspaper article describing how Mrs. Sinico was killed by a slow-moving train while crossing a track at night, possibly in an inebriated state. Instead of giving Duffy an acute sense of sorrow, her "commonplace vulgar death" as a drunk "revolted him," as he "saw the squalid tract of her vice, miserable and malodorous" (97).

It is not until later that evening that, while taking a walk, Duffy begins to ask himself whether "he had denied her life and happiness" (98) and therefore contributed to her possible suicide. All this seems to make "A Painful Case" an adultery narrative on the order of Tolstoy's *Anna Karenina* who also dies on a train track struck by a train—but in Joyce's story there is *no* adultery, and it appears to be the refusal of adultery that causes the tragedy.

Why was Duffy unable to love Mrs. Sinico? This is where the story becomes even more complicated because we are given a single clue that is never discussed or explained but nonetheless turns the story upside down. Two months after breaking up with her, Duffy wrote in his private journal his thoughts that "Love between man and man is impossible because there must not be sexual intercourse and friendship between man and woman is impossible because there must be sexual intercourse" (94). Was Duffy unable to respond to Mrs. Sinico because he is a latent or closeted homosexual? Except for that single revelation in Duffy's papers, the narration tells us nothing more about his sexual orientation, and particularly fails to mention whether he spoke to Mrs. Sinico about it during the lengthy conversation right before their break-up.

Why would Joyce keep the cause of Duffy's refusal to love Mrs. Sinico so mysterious? Two scandals involving Irishmen rocked Ireland at the time of the story's narration: the adulterous affair of the politician Charles Stewart Parnell and the sodomy trial and conviction of Oscar Wilde. Both adultery and homosexuality were highly charged forbidden relationships in English-speaking countries in the early 20th century, and almost impossible to write about openly—which explains why Joyce published his 1922 *Ulysses* in France rather than in Ireland or England, and why *Dubliners* could not have been published had he treated this version of James Duffy's story openly in "A Painful Case."

"Ivy Day in the Committee Room"

The progress from childhood to adolescence to adulthood in the themes of *Dubliners* takes another turn in this story, which deals not with a single protagonist or narrator but with a collective group of men who work as canvassers during a Dublin election campaign. They get together on a cold and rainy evening in the "committee room" of the Nationalist party. Some of them wear an ivy leaf in their lapels, setting the date of the story precisely as October 6, 1902, the anniversary of the death of the great Irish political leader, Charles Stewart Parnell, who died in 1891 after the revelation of his adultery ended his career.

The story's plot is simple: all day the men have been trying to stir people to vote for their candidate, and they now hope they will be paid for their work. They are tired, wet, and cold, sitting in a room lit only by a small fire and a couple of candles. They talk about their candidates and their political differences—conversations not easily sorted out by readers unfamiliar with the Irish politics of the day. A basket full of bottles of stout is delivered while they wait, and as the topic is turned to the celebrant of the day, one of the men is asked to recite a poem he wrote about Parnell's death. The poem's moving rendition ends the story with a burst of applause, silence, and more stout.

But if the crux of the story is simple, its point is larger and more subtle. Politics mattered intensely in Ireland, a country with a complicated political situation, wide-spread poverty, talk of favoritism and corruption, as well as of hopes for progress and improvement. What this really means, however, is expressed in the condition of the men who appear to have families but no regular jobs: some are missing teeth, have splotches on their faces, leaking shoes, and not enough money to pay their rents. "I expect to find the bailiffs in the hall when I go home," one of the men says, clearly worried about a rent collector coming to arrest him if he hasn't paid (105). Politics is talk, we see here, both exalted and committed, empty and deceptive, and sometimes almost promising salvation as the honorable commitment of Joyce's hero, Charles Stewart Parnell, did for so many Irishmen in his day, before the Catholic Church's attack on his adultery brought him down. But Joyce also underlines politics and the talk that informs and supports it by showing us the stakes in the lives of struggling, ordinary men.

"A Mother"

After the social focus of the previous story, "A Mother" appears at first glance to take us back to such earlier family stories as "Eveline" and "The Boarding House." But this story also has a social focus—although on the world of art and entertainment rather than politics—and it actually gains much illumination by comparing its theme with issues raised in "Ivy Day in the Committee Room."

The reason "A Mother" appears so different is because it begins by giving us a somewhat unflattering introduction to a single character, a Mrs. Kearney, who is described as a strong woman skilled at making sure that everything in her life will serve her advantage. She marries a dull but stable and responsible man, makes sure her daughter gets a good education, shrewdly supports the Irish Revival, and when approached about having her daughter Kathleen serve as the piano accompanist at a series of upcoming concerts, she enthusiastically agrees. A contract is signed stating Kathleen's salary for her participation, and Mrs. Kearney works hard to promote the event only to find it is poorly organized and attracts little attendance. This alarms her sufficiently that she seeks out the concert managers at the beginning of the last concert to demand that her daughter be paid then and there, which is done only grudgingly and partially.

Before the second part of the concert she asks for the remaining pay again, and is told that the managerial committee will discuss the matter at a later time. When she argues with the men and threatens to withdraw her daughter from the concert, she is publicly reprimanded and denounced ("You might have some sense of decency, said Mr Holohan [. . . .] I thought you were a lady" [127]). Having received no satisfaction, Mrs. Kearney, along with her daughter and husband, storm out.

The story is narrated in a way that makes the condemnation of Mrs. Kearney by everyone at the concert seem entirely justified, and it is therefore not surprising that critics and readers may feel the same way. But it is here that a possible split in response should be considered, especially if we hark back to the question of pay as it is raised in "Ivy Day in the Committee Room." In that story, it seems outrageous that the manifestly poor campaign canvassers might not be paid for their work on a cold and rainy day by politicians who profess to promote and protect the interests of their electorate. Consequently, the reader would be obliged to judge such an outcome to the story quite harshly. But "A Mother" reminds us that the production of art is also work, also labor, and that singers and pianists must also eat and earn a living with their work. So why should the story's mother be judged harshly for demanding that her daughter's contract be honored and her work paid?

The story appears to foreground both the necessity of treating art as an economic enterprise as well as an aesthetic one, and the problem of gender equality, that women have a right to be paid for their work as surely as men do. The narrative's negative descriptions of Mrs. Kearney have, in a sense, pre-judged her in a way that makes it difficult for the reader to judge her demand for her daughter's pay without pre-judgment, or prejudice.

"Grace"

Like the two previous stories, "Grace" offers a focus on Dublin's social life, this time with religion in an apparently central role. But a closer look reveals that—like "Ivy Day" and "A Mother"—the theme buried under the actions and discussions is once again money. This is difficult to divine beginning with the mystery of why a man who turns out to be a Mr. Kernan fell down the steps of a lavatory in a bar he visited with two men who are never clearly identified. Was the fall an accident—perhaps caused by drinking too much—or did it have something to do with the occupation of one of the men, Mr. Harford, who appears to work for a possibly unscrupulous moneylender as a "muscle" or enforcer? Did Kernan fail to pay a debt and was he therefore pushed down the stairs to teach him a lesson and to threaten him with future violence if he fails to pay up?

None of this is made clear in the story, and the focus soon turns to Mr. Power, a friend who kindly offers to take Kernan home to a wife who has been waiting anxiously for her husband to bring her money so that she can feed her family. Power appears to have some sense of what may be going on and therefore arranges with some friends to stage what we would now call an "intervention," a plan to try to get Kernan to face his drinking problem—presumably the cause of his debts and bankrupted condition—by attending a religious temperance retreat. The men all meet in Kernan's bedroom where he is recuperating, and turn the discussion to religion, Jesuits, and the preaching of Catholic priests, leading up to a casual mention of the retreat they are planning to attend. Kernan, a Catholic only by marriage, has to be coaxed into joining them, and the story ends with a kindly sermon by Father Purdon at the retreat, urging the men gently to seek to correct their faults and failings and put their accounts with God in order.

The story ends there without letting us know if the retreat worked, although we are predisposed to doubt it. Father Purdon's account is careful not to condemn but only urges and coaxes, and in a sense, the entire narration has done just that: urge and coax us not to be too hard on Mr. Kernan and to look at the whole business in a positive and encouraging light. The problem is that Kernan's behavior victimizes his family and others, as we will learn later in *Ulysses*, where we find out that Mr. Fogarty, a kindly grocer to whom the Kernans owe huge amounts of money, is never repaid and consequently suffers bankruptcy. Money and debts are ugly topics, to be sure, but the story reminds us that they have enormous moral and ethical implications with respect to how they are handled and treated in society. Society, like this narration, prefers not to look at them too closely or deal with them too directly.

"The Dead"

And so we come to the last story in the collection, the ominously titled "The Dead," which, like "A Mother," appears to be centered on family—in this case the extended family of Gabriel Conroy, his wife Gretta, his aunts Kate and Julia, and their niece, Mary Jane.

There is also romance in the story, or perhaps its opposite, as the maid Lily would see it when she tells Gabriel Conroy that "The men that is now is only all palaver and what they can get out of you" (154)—an effective retort in the event Gabriel might have contemplated making a pass at her. An even more complicated romantic problem besets the married Gabriel and Gretta at the end. And like the previous three *Dubliners* stories, "The Dead" brings up larger social issues, brilliantly weaving politics, art, and religion together with questions of gender, age, and race.

The plot centers on a holiday party the elderly Morkan sisters and their niece Mary Jane host annually for friends, family, and members of Dublin's musical society in which the Morkans have played, and continue to play, a role. There are conversations about music and musical performances, all intertwined with a variety of conflicts. Art and politics create problems between Gabriel Conroy and Miss Ivors, a strong supporter of the Irish Revival who taunts him for writing about Browning's poetry in a conservative newspaper and for preferring to travel to the Continent to improve his French and German rather than to the Aran Isles in western Ireland to retrieve Ireland's lost Gaelic language.

In general, the story foregrounds the pleasant atmosphere of the party, while treating conflicts between the characters as minor distractions. It is therefore up to the reader to pay attention to the significant stakes in some of the conflicts that erupt. One of the most poignant concerns Aunt Julia, who was recently dismissed from the church choir in which she had sung for many years as the result of a historical papal edict barring women from singing at Catholic services. Julia's sister Kate is extremely angry about this but is quickly silenced by her niece, and the party continues with dinner. Julia had earlier sung a song so beautifully that the narration calls her voice "strong and clear," notes that she misses not even "the smallest of the grace notes," and says that to "follow the voice, without looking at the singer's face, was to feel and share the excitement of swift and secure flight" (168). Clearly, Kate is right, and that Julia is a gifted singer who has suffered a grave injustice at the hands of the Church. But both the narration and the characters in the story gloss over this in a move the reader could, and should, construe as both sexist and ageist. A second small incident that repeats this pattern occurs when a guest named Freddy Malins mentions a "negro chieftain" currently singing at the

Gaiety pantomime, "who had one of the finest tenor voice he had ever heard" (172). When no one reacts to this, Freddy asks sharply if people assume the tenor cannot have a great voice. "Is it because he's only a black?" (173). Art is fraught with politics, the reader can infer from these incidents, where at a congenial evening musical dinner party old women and blacks are denied recognition and respect for extraordinary talent on the grounds of gender, age, and race.

The story's narration brushes these issues aside, and the party ends well. However, one more incident of the slighting of a woman is raised when after the party Gabriel Conroy is moved by seeing his wife on a stair listening to a romantic song. This stirs romantic feelings in him, and on their return to their hotel room, he approaches Gretta only to find that the song reminded her of a young tubercular man who used to sing that tune, and who once stood beneath her window in the rain declaring his love for her shortly before he died. Gabriel has played such a major role not only at the party, but also in his family's entire life, that his focus is chiefly on his own feelings, including his own romantic feelings, rather than those of others, including his wife. As a result, when Gretta describes being courted by her young lover, a scene with resonances of "Romeo and Juliet," Gabriel is shaken and for the first time feels overshadowed and demeaned. "He saw himself as a ludicrous figure, acting as a pennyboy for his aunts," and as "a piteous fatuous fellow" who had been "idealizing his own clownish lusts" (191). Joyce was a great admirer of Henrik Ibsen's "A Doll's House," a drama with a similar marital dynamic in which the husband must confront the fact that he is not the center of his wife's existence and that he scarcely knows her after years of marriage.

In "The Dead" Joyce covers important social and political issues in the Ireland of his time, while weaving them into a series of intimate familial, personal, and even marital relationships. As in previous stories, the reader is obliged to work against the narration at times, to see in the story of a merry holiday party dominated by a patriarchal figure, leading and caring for his family, a more hidden story of women ignored, discounted, and displaced with other concerns. Perhaps some justice has been achieved when, at the story's end, Gabriel is awake after Gretta goes to sleep, thinking and feeling that his soul "had approached that region where dwell the vast hosts of the dead" (194).

3

A Portrait of the Artist as a Young Man

It is difficult to pin down exactly when Joyce began writing his first novel, *A Portrait of the Artist as a Young Man.* By some accounts its first draft was a sketch produced in 1904, although the first attempts at the manuscript that became its prelude—titled *Stephen Hero*—might have appeared as early as 1903. No complete manuscript of *Stephen Hero* survived, although Joyce might have completed it by 1906 and begun sending it to publishers. After receiving a series of rejections, however, he nearly destroyed it in a fit of frustration. His friend and publisher, Sylvia Beach, later reported that Joyce shoved the manuscript into a burning stove and his wife Nora rescued as many pages as she could, burning her hands in the process. Joyce then began a new version of the novel in 1907 and in early 1914, with the help of his new admirer Ezra Pound, and his later patron Harriet Shaw Weaver, *A Portrait of the Artist as a Young Man* began serial publication in the journal *The Egoist.* The first printed edition appeared in 1916, and thanks to Pound's support, it received a generally enthusiastic reception in spite of some criticism of its treatment of religion.

The stories of *Dubliners* gloss only occasional moments and experiences in Joyce's life, but *Portrait* is based more consistently on his educational experiences: first at the boarding school called Clongowes Wood College in County Kildare, followed by his time at the Jesuit high school of Belvedere in Dublin, and his subsequent studies at University College, Dublin. Critic Morris Beja's biography documents Joyce's experiences at these institutions that found their way into *Portrait*: including his unjust punishment with a pandybat at Clongowes, the annual retreat and the prizes he won at Belvedere, and the romantic moment when he saw a young woman wading in a stream that revealed to him his vocation as an artist (*James Joyce: A Literary Life*). Joyce also enjoyed other experiences in those years that are not recorded in *Portrait*, or in the later *Ulysses*, such as his meeting with the distinguished poet William Butler Yeats, which took place in London while Joyce was on his way to study medicine in Paris.

What transitions does Joyce implement in moving from the short stories of *Dubliners* to the novelistic form of *A Portrait of the Artist as a Young Man*? The book's title makes it clear that its protagonist is a young artist. Like *Dubliners*, it begins in childhood, although at an earlier time of life than any found in "The Sisters," "An Encounter," or "Araby." As it proceeds, its narrative follows *Dubliners* in progressing systematically from an account of younger years to adolescence to young adulthood, but in the single figure of a protagonist named Stephen Dedalus, rather than in the series of boys and young persons found in the stories. The name Dedalus evokes "Daedalus," the mythological artist and artisan mentioned by Homer, and thereby points to the importance of Classicism as a feature of Joyce's art, a characteristic even more prominently displayed in the title of *Ulysses*. The Greek Daedalus sought to escape his confinement on the island of Crete by fashioning wings for himself and his son Icarus in order to fly across the sea. In Joyce's novel, this mythical story will hint at Stephen Dedalus's hope to leave Ireland for the Continent to pursue his artistic vocation.

Portrait confines itself to Stephen's years from childhood through adolescence, and although he returns as a figure in Joyce's *Ulysses*, we never learn how his life continues beyond his 20s. The more dramatic difference between *Dubliners* and *Portrait* is not thematic, however, but stylistic. The childhood stories of *Dubliners* are narrated from an arguably adult perspective, but the opening sentence of *Portrait* tells us how "a moocow coming down along the road met a nicens little boy named baby tuckoo" (7). This language suggests that we are told this in the vocabulary and syntax of a small boy, but the narration continues in the third person and gradually matures as the boy matures. This symbiosis of stylistic and chronological maturation is, in a sense, the hallmark of *A Portrait*, as it transforms artistic awareness and ambition from a thematic characteristic of a young boy and young man into a stylistic enactment in its prose.

Before looking at both the thematic and stylistic developments in *Portrait*, it may be helpful to briefly examine *Stephen Hero* since this work also sheds light on the way Joyce decided to shape his revised version of Stephen Dedalus. Only a few critics have taken *Stephen Hero* seriously as significant in its own right, notably Joyce scholar Michael Gillespie who argues that "it would be a mistake to relegate it to an ancillary position in Joyce's canon—either as a piece of juvenilia or as the rough sketch of later work" (*Reading the Book of Himself*, 43). He points out a difference in the focus of the two texts, with *Stephen Hero* devoted more to representing day-to-events rather than the mental ruminations of the protagonist. Critic Patrick Parrinder also attributes to *Stephen Hero* moments of "painstaking realistic narrative" (*James Joyce*, 32), pointing to one episode in particular that Joyce omitted from *A Portrait*. This is a painful conversation between Stephen and his mother, who is tending her very ill daughter. She comes into the room where he is sitting at the piano in the gloom of a late afternoon and asks him a question—"Do you know anything about the body?" (*Stephen Hero* 163). Her "excited face was crimson," the narration tells us, and her voice is described as the "voice of a terrified human being." Her concern is that "[t]here's some matter coming away from the hole in Isabel's . . . stomach," but she cannot bring herself to be give a more specific name to the unmentionable body part, able to identify it only as "The hole . . . the hole we all have . . . here."

There is a poignancy in this scene of a mother and son needing to communicate about a painful topic with some inevitable embarrassment, and critics can only guess that the reason it is omitted from *Portrait* is for just that reason—it is simply too dramatic and "raw," as Parrinder describes it, to fit the narrative and stylistic spirit of understatement that characterizes the later work. But even so, this scene harks back to a feature already discussed in the stories of *Dubliners*—namely its provocation to prod the reader into trying to figure out what is going on, what the language is suppressing and why. The realism of distinctive moments like those in the scene above continues in the sharp detail of many ensuing scenes of *Stephen Hero*, and its overall narrative lays the groundwork for the story of artistic development that will be the central focus of *Portrait*. It offers an insight into Stephen's relationship with family and friends, the contributions and trials found in the process of education, the difficulties posed by the strictures of religion, and the liberating but also intellectually challenging commitment to a life devoted to art.

As we proceed chapter by chapter, *Portrait's* central focus will be on the relationship between Stephen's familial and social development as a thematic topic and the development of the narrative language and style as it reflects his emotional and intellectual development. This focus on development places *Portrait* in the tradition of the *Bildungsroman,* a novelistic genre that is generally traced back to the

18th century and to the work of the German writer Johann Wolfgang von Goethe titled *Wilhelm Meister*. In his discussion of *Portrait,* Joyce critic Breon Mitchell points out that the *Bildungsroman* has a specific agenda: it aims to show how a young man's experiences can make him "a well-rounded individual who is both knowledgeable and wise," and how he can best be prepared "to take his meaningful and rightful place in society" (63).

This process entails an exploration of the effects of upbringing, education, and cultural influences that shape a person's outlook, values, and ambitions. But by its title, *A Portrait of the Artist* also places itself in the more specific category of the *Künstlerroman,* the genre that complicates the development narrative by making it the story of the genesis and growth of the artist and the artistic imagination. We will certainly see this in young Stephen Dedalus's conflicts with friends and institutions, his yearnings and needs, his work to make sense of his condition and that of the world surrounding him, and his reflections on the results of these efforts—not only in the production of but also in his conceptualization of art.

But as noted previously, Joyce goes beyond the *Künstlerroman* tradition and does something quite extraordinary by making the telling of the artistic development *performative*, as it were—that is, he has the narration act out or demonstrate the artistic development it is discussing in the language and style of the narration itself. In a curious way, when reading *Portrait*, we have the sense that the artist's development or *Bildung* has indeed been completed in a highly successful way, given how his story is told. This will require a double focus as we take up each of the chapters of *Portrait*. At the same time that we learn of Stephen's experiences, we also need to explore the language in which they are presented to us. One benefit of this double perspective is that it further complicates the work generically, by giving its novelistic prose a highly poetic dimension that requires us to function not only as readers but also as literary critics. Here is what Stephen seems to observe as he walks and talks with his friend Cranly: "The park trees were heavy with rain and rain fell still and ever in the lake, lying grey like a shield. A game of swans flew there and the water and the shore beneath were fouled with their greenwhite slime" (*A Portrait of the Artist as a Young Man*, 228). The scene is factual in one respect yet nuanced by words and concepts: rain that is "heavy" "still" and falling "ever," creating a metaphoric "shield" on the lake. The swans that we may picture as flying gracefully over water and shore also function as living creatures rather than mere images with the "greenwhite slime" they deposit over the water. This is not mere storytelling but artistic and poetic in its style.

Chapter I

The first chapter of *Portrait* tells, in four sections, the story of Stephen Dedalus's early childhood with each part organized around a trauma that the young boy experiences. The first one appears to focus on the period right after infancy, when the little boy is old enough to hear childhood stories but before he goes to school. It is unclear why he hides under the table or why his mother says, "O, Stephen will apologise" (8). But his functional "aunt" Dante's elaboration, "O, if not, the eagles will come and pull out his eyes" makes it clear that the little boy has done something punishable that ends up creating a traumatic experience for him.

The second section shows Stephen at the private Jesuit boarding school—one that Joyce himself attended—Clongowes Wood College, located about 40 miles from Dublin in County Kildare. If that section has an autobiographical basis, we can judge Stephen's age at this point to be around seven years old. Joyce biographer Richard Ellmann tells us that when Joyce arrived at Clongowes, he was asked how old he was and his reply was "[h]alf past six, a phrase that became for some time his school nickname" (*James Joyce,* 27).

The trauma of this first Clongowes section is not actually represented, but we learn indirectly that a classmate had pushed little Stephen into the water of a cold ditch, an experience that landed him in the infirmary the next day with chills and fever. This event appears to have taken place before Christmas, the time of the third section, when Stephen is home celebrating the holiday at a family dinner attended by his father's friend, the Irish nationalist Mr. Casey. The lovely dinner turns into a debacle when the conversation turns to Irish politics, and Stephen is obliged to witness an altercation between the religious Dante and Mr. Casey. The conflict Stephen sees played out operates on two levels—between family and friends, but also on the national level, where the Catholic Church's attack on the nationalist Charles Stewart Parnell created a historical crisis in Ireland.

After this devastating Christmas dinner, Stephen returns to Clongowes where he experiences another trauma, this time not at the hands of a classmate but from a priest who visits the classroom and punishes the boy by striking his hand with a bat, presumably because he assumed that Stephen broke his glasses to get out of school work.

This fourth section ends triumphantly, with little Stephen deciding to get justice by reporting the unfair punishment to the school's rector. His classmates cheer when he returns and tells them of his success.

When the next chapter begins, things are not going so well with the Dedalus family, and we see a pattern that perdures throughout *Portrait*—that of having chapters end on a highly positive and encouraging note only to have things brought back down to the dismal earth at the beginning of the next.

The infancy section of Chapter I starts with the standard beginning of fairy tales: "Once upon a time and a very good time it was there was a moocow coming down along the road" (7). A moment later we learn that this was what the little boy was hearing, a story told to him by his father. The narration is in the third-person, but as the father is described, we realize that the narrator's vocabulary is that of a small child. "[H]is father looked at him through a glass: he had a hairy face." The little boy does not yet know the words "monocle," "spectacle," "glasses," "mustache" or "beard." His toddler state is further demonstrated by the observation "[w]hen you wet the bed first it is warm then it gets cold," describing what he actually experiences when he wets the bed. But a few lines later, the little boy seems to have matured a bit. When he describes Dante's maroon and green brushes, he understands that the colors are symbolic and is even able to name Michael Davitt and Parnell, the men they symbolize, even if he does not yet understand their political agendas. He then describes some apparent neighbors, the Vances, and their daughter Eileen with whom he appears to have a close friendship—"When they were grown up he was going to marry Eileen" (8). And it is then that we hear Stephen's mother telling him he must apologize, and Dante's threat that the eagles will pull out his eyes if he does not. This is the gist of the infancy introduction, but it also repeats songs, melodies, and rhymes that he hears, about a wild rose that blossoms, the sailor's hornpipe "*Tralala lala*," and the ominous rhyme of "Pull out his eyes,/ Apologise." This is the little boy's first encounter with art, we surmise, with music and poetry both lovely and dangerous. We have also learned his name—"O, Stephen will apologise"—and a sketch of family. It includes a father who tells stories, a mother who plays the piano, an Uncle Charles, and Dante (a live-in friend who functions like a German *Tante* or aunt), and their clapping when Stephen dances to his mother's piano music.

The skillful deployment of the narrative language in this section lets the *Künstlerroman* begin with a literary performance that enacts

Stephen's childhood maturation—not only in the details of the narrative but also in the language and manner in which it is represented.

The first Clongowes section of the chapter opens on a football field where a game is in progress. But Stephen does not really play, "feigning to run now and then" (8). "He felt his body small and weak amid the throng of players and his eyes were weak and watery." It is a chilly evening and "his hands were bluish with cold" (9) and "he shivered as if he had cold slimy water next to his skin" (10). This turns out not to be a metaphor but reference to a recent experience. "That was mean of Wells to shoulder him into the square ditch because he would not swop his little snuffbox for Wells's seasoned hacking chestnut."

This narrative gives us a sketch of Stephen's life at the boarding school where he suffers from both physical and social vulnerability. He is not athletic, making him a target for bullies. On this particular evening, his mind continually goes back to his comfortable home in Dublin, where he remembers "Mother was sitting at the fire with Dante waiting for Brigid to bring in the tea." This memory is sparked by his wish "to lie on the hearthrug before the fire, leaning his head upon his hands" and think of some poetic sentences in his spelling book.

Stephen is clearly a shy, but bright little boy attuned to words and poetry, less interested in the white and red roses of the houses of York and Lancaster as portrayed in history books, than in the wild rose that blossomed in the rhymes of his infancy. He also shows a philosophical bent, thinking about the universe—"was there anything round the universe to show where it stopped" (16)—and about the nature of God.

On this day at Clongowes, Stephen shivers as he gets ready for bed, and by the time he climbs under the cold white sheets, he is "shaking and trembling" (19). It is his classmate Fleming who had noticed that Stephen was not well, and who tells him the next morning to stay in bed, fetching the prefect who will arrange for Stephen to go to the infirmary. Wells, alarmed that he will get in trouble for having pushed Stephen into the cold ditch water apologizes to him: "It was only for cod. I'm sorry" (21). In the infirmary, Stephen confronts his mortality. "He might die before his mother came" (24) he thinks, and imagines that "they would carry the coffin out of the chapel slowly and he would be buried in the little graveyard," making Wells sorry for what he had done. These morbid thoughts are eased a bit by the talk and riddles of a fellow named Athy, who shares his infirmary room. But as Stephen drifts off to sleep, he has a vision of a multitude of people awaiting a ship at a harbor, emitting a wail of sorrow at the news that "Parnell! Parnell! He is dead!" (27)

This section offers a vivid view of young Stephen's juvenile personality, his physical and social vulnerabilities, the pain of his emotional separation from his warm home and family, and his lively mind and vivid imagination processing words, stories, and information, even as he has to deal with the consequences of a very difficult day in his young life. The episode also details the consequences of conflict—a childish response to an unwillingness to make a trade, which becomes the prelude to the much larger sense of conflict that is rocking the Ireland of his day, and one that comes to a climax in the devastating argument between Dante and Mr. Casey in the next section of this chapter.

The Christmas dinner scene begins promisingly enough with a great fire warming the room, the chandelier trimmed with ivy, and the family waiting for the servants to bring in "big dishes covered with their heavy metal covers" (27). It is as though Stephen's dreamy wish of a happy home while at Clongowes is being fulfilled. But the lovely dinner will be overlaid by the escalating conflict among Dante, Simon Dedalus, and his friend Mr. Casey, over the Church's role in bringing down the Irish patriot Charles Stewart Parnell. The narration presents this scene in the third person from an adult perspective, but we are reminded that little Stephen is watching and listening to it all, but unable to sort out what the conflict is about. He knows Mr. Casey spent time in prison for "making speeches from a wagonette" (37), and he remembers a Sergeant O'Neill once coming to his house to speak nervously to his father about Mr. Casey. Yet he wonders why there would be a conflict if Mr. Casey "was for Ireland and Parnell and so was his father: and so was Dante too."

But there definitely is a conflict. Mr. Dedalus calls priests "Sons of bitches!" and accuses them of having betrayed Parnell and destroyed him "like rats in a sewer" (34). And Mr. Casey aims an ultimate blasphemy at Dante by insisting that if God and religion come before everything, then "no God for Ireland!" and "Away with God!" (39). The dinner ends with Stephen raising "his terrorstricken face" to see his father's eyes full of tears (39). Yet, the lesson Stephen takes away from this quarrel stands him in good stead when he returns to Clongowes, and is unjustly beaten with a pandybat by the prefect for having broken his glasses, presumably to get out of school work ("Broke my glasses! An old schoolboy trick!") (50).

The Church and its priests are capable of oppression on both large and small scales, it appears. When his classmate Fleming, who was also beaten for being a lazy, idle loafer, defends Stephen and encourages him to "go up and tell the rector on him" (52), timid little Stephen somehow musters the courage to do just that. He may not be consciously imitating Parnell, or even his father and Mr. Casey, and he knows that his protest may backfire and result in more pandybatting. But, all the same, his small burst of courage appears to have been obliquely underwritten by the witnessed Christmas dinner fight. In Stephen's childhood experience, the topic of politics has been transformed from narrative and story into action, conflict, oppression, and revolt, or, at least, a response to oppression.

Chapter II

In the second chapter, Stephen's transition from childhood into adolescence is accompanied by a problematic change in the social state of his family. The narration presents this with some subtlety, first by opening the limited horizon of home and school into a broader scene of Dublin and its environs, with Stephen accompanying his Uncle Charles to markets and parks, playing at adventure battles with his friend Aubrey Mills, and riding with a milkman on his route into the pastoral surroundings of the suburbs where "the cows were at grass" (63). He listens to his father and grand-uncle discuss politics, focused more on the language than on the social issues. "Words which he did not understand he said over and over to himself till he had learned them by heart: and through them he had glimpses of the real world about him" (62).

The artistic ambition at the heart of the *Künstlerroman* is in Stephen's heart, preparing him for "the great part which he felt awaited him" in his life. And it is art that gives him the first stirring of romance through the language of a "ragged translation" of *The Count of Monte Cristo* that he reads in the evenings. The tension at the core of this time in his life is that as his soul reaches upward, as he longs to achieve a transformation into some greater version of himself, the material life around him disintegrates. This threatens to deprive him of the advantages of class and affluence that might have held great promise for him in the first chapter.

Scholar Morris Beja reports that Joyce's family also suffered a "declining financial state in 1891" (6), requiring a series of moves to poorer and poorer housing. The *Portrait* narration conveys the effects of this change by embedding Stephen's still-unclear and struggling thoughts and feelings into highly precise renderings of the material conditions of the world around him. In his fantasies, he pictures an encounter with an undefined female "image" that he envisions he would "meet quietly as if they had known each other and had made their tryst" (65). But his reality is peopled by figures like his father's friend, Mike Flynn, with his "stubblecovered face" lit by "mild lustreless blue eyes," and hands with long swollen and stained fingers that roll tobacco into cigarettes with grains and fibers falling back into the pouch (61). The narration offers an explanation of the deterioration of the material surroundings only through Stephen's struggling and unclear sense of what is going on. "In a vague way he understood that his father was in trouble and that this was the reason why he himself had not been sent back to Clongowes" (64).

Later, on the first night in a new "half furnished uncarpeted" house whose parlor fire does not draw and whose bare floors are muddy from the shoes of the moving men, Stephen hears his father deliver a "long and incoherent monologue. He understood little or nothing of it at first but he became slowly aware that his father had enemies and that some fight was going to take place" (65).

Visits to his extended family in the city offer little comfort in the weeks that follow, for his relatives too have their problems. They can only dream of the beauty of the pantomime by looking at pictures in the newspaper. The family includes an infirm member described as a "feeble creature like a monkey (68), whose whining voice mistakes Stephen for a female 'Josephine.' No wonder Stephen is bitter: angry at himself not only for his "restless foolish impulses," but also at "the change of fortune which was reshaping the world about him into a vision of squalor and insincerity" (67).

But curiously, Clongowes re-emerges in this chapter to give Stephen some critical help at this desperate time. He overhears his father tell his mother that he has bumped into someone who will arrange to get Stephen into Belvedere, a Dublin Jesuit school of much higher caliber than the Christian brothers' schools the underprivileged are obliged to attend. The narration only describes what Stephen hears, so it is not until the end that we, and presumably Stephen, can infer that it was Father Conmee, the rector to whom Stephen had complained about being unfairly pandy-batted, who tells the father that the incident gave him and Father Dolan, who beat the boys, a "famous laugh" over little Stephen's protest—"Ha! Ha! Ha!" (72). We are not given Stephen's response to hearing this story, yet can imagine that it all but destroyed his childhood moment of heroism.

But Stephen does well at Belvedere, where his reputation for essay writing gets him elected chairman of the gymnasium, and earns him a role in the annual Whitsuntide play. However, the oppressive nature of Catholicism that broke into conflict at the Christmas dinner some years before has not entirely gone away. It surfaces in a memory evoked in Stephen when his classmate Heron strikes him playfully on the leg with a cane. Near the end of his first term, Stephen had apparently been reproved by one of his teachers for inadvertently making a "heretical" statement in the phrase of an essay he wrote. At a later encounter with a group of classmates that includes Heron, the fellows decide to test Stephen's orthodoxy with a set of charged questions, asking him to name the "greatest writer," and then also "the best poet" (80). He passes the first question by naming Cardinal Newman, but his answer of "Byron" to the second earns him a beating on his legs with Heron's cane, and a demand that he admit that Byron, whom the boys consider an immoral "heretic," "was no good" (82).

Stephen does not concede and even allows the "cowardice and cruelty" of his classmates to pass into oblivion without resentment in the aftermath. But the incident resurfaces his conflict with the oppressive character of the Church, this time related specifically to his personal passion for and avocation of art. Joyce here focuses the challenges to be overcome by the emerging artist in the *Künstlerroman* on ongoing conflict with the effects of Irish Catholicism—not only on politics but also on art. The greatest challenge remains, however, and it will concern the issue of the adolescent's emerging sexual feelings and inclinations, which will dramatically evoke the shamed response produced by Stephen's religious retreat in the upcoming Chapter III.

However,Stephen's attention to females begins in Chapter II—very sweetly—on the way home from a children's party at Harold's Cross. A girl playfully dances up and down the tram's steps as "her glance travelled to his corner, flattering, taunting, searching, exciting his heart" (69). They appear not to speak, conversing only with looks and movements, but she clearly stirs some latent romantic impulses in Stephen and he thinks "I could hold her and kiss her" (70), although he does not. What he does do is transform the experience and his feelings into art on the next day, with a poem dedicated "To E___ C____", whose initials, we learn in *Stephen Hero*, refer to a young woman named Emma Clery. A somewhat tense conversation Stephen has with

Emma in that work is followed by the appearance of a woman with a glazed face, wearing a black straw hat who appears to be a prostitute.

Later, in *Portrait*, Stephen undergoes a transition from innocent romantic sensations provoked by Emma to "wasting fires of lust" that have him moan like some "baffled prowling beast" (99) as he wanders the "maze of narrow and dirty streets" (100) of Dublin's red light district. This transition is separated by a series of family experiences including the night of the Whitsuntide play.

Before the play begins, Heron tells Stephen "We saw her" (77), referring to a young woman accompanying Stephen's family who have come to see his performance. "*And what part does Stephen take, Mr Dedalus?*" Heron reports her as saying to Stephen's father, and Stephen's thoughts confirm that the young woman is indeed Emma, the girl with whom he had shared the tram ride at Harold's Cross, the one who inspired his poem, and whom he has not seen again in the last two years.

The play, including Stephen's performance, goes off splendidly, and when it is over, his "nerves cried for some further adventure" (85), presumably with the young woman who had come to see him perform. But he is devastated to find that she is gone after the play, and he leaves his family to run off in a swirl "of wounded pride and fallen hope and baffled desire" (86). His first romantic experience has ended in abandonment.

Further degradations of his family life will follow with a trip to Cork to sell his father's property at auction, a downturn reprieved with a brief financial family renaissance when Stephen's exhibition and essay prize money allows him to restore a brief affluence and elegance to his family. But this reprieve deteriorates as quickly as it began, "How foolish his aim had been!" (98). And now the "savage desire" and "secret riots" (97-98) that had caused him to commit mortal sins of lechery in his heart and his imagination are translated into actual wanderings into the brothel area. There he will follow a young woman dressed in a long pink gown into her room and, unwilling or unable to kiss her, she imposes a kiss whose pressure is to him "darker than the swoon of sin" (101).

Chapter III

Throughout Chapter II the style of the narration struggles with the intense emotional conflict that adolescence and the changing conditions of his family life impose on Stephen by alternating objective surroundings with his internal ruminations. His feelings can only be described in simple terms, and represented with simple details. "His very brain was sick and powerless," we are told as he listens to his father try to recapture old friendships and pleasures on the depressing trip to Cork. "He could scarcely interpret the letters of the signboards of the shops. By his monstrous way of life he seemed to have put himself beyond the limits of reality" (92). This is followed by a poignant moment when Stephen tries to recapture reality with the simplest and most purely factual statements he can muster: "I am Stephen Dedalus. I am walking beside my father whose name is Simon Dedalus. We are in Cork, in Ireland. Cork is a city" (92). Joyce turns Stephen's dilemma inside out here, by having wholly unemotional language convey emotional anguish precisely in its reversal.

Chapter III moves in a different direction. In its opening we encounter Stephen in a schoolroom, working equations on the page of a notebook. But the narration enters his thoughts which roam almost aimlessly around his moral life, the contrast between his acute sense of sin and his hypocritically pious outer life. Even as he views with contempt the Sunday church-goers who repel him with "the sickly smell of the cheap hairoil with which they had anointed their heads" (104), he is strangely enchanted by an image of the Blessed Virgin Mary, whose "eyes seemed to regard him with mild pity" and whose holiness shines like "a strange light glowing faintly upon her frail flesh" that makes him wish to be her knight (105).

This conflicted inner life of adolescence is soon subjected to an intervention clearly designed by the Church to address it in a most powerful way with the sermons of an annual religious retreat. The sermons are cleverly designed to encourage the teenage boys to "examine the state of our conscience, to reflect on the mysteries of holy religion and to understand better why we are here in this world" (109). By appealing to the four last things—"death, judgment, hell, and heaven"—the boys will be encouraged and frightened into considering how to "save our immortal souls" because "[a]ll else is worthless" (110). Instead of reporting or describing Father Arnall's first sermon, the narration offers it verbatim at length, as Stephen hears it. A "faint glimmer of fear began to pierce the fog of his mind" (111) and by the second sermon this "became a terror of spirit as the hoarse voice of the preacher blew death into his soul" (112). This second sermon appears to flow from Stephen's thoughts and feelings into the words he hears, "And this day will come, shall come, must come; the day of death and the day of judgment" (114), and its effect is powerful. "Every word of it was for him. Against his sin, foul and secret, the whole wrath of God was aimed," he thinks. As he walks home, a young girl's voice evokes, if only in his mind, how Emma would judge the "brutelike lust" that had "torn and trampled upon her innocence" (115). His shame prompts him to imagine that he could reverse his degraded state by fantasizing that "he stood near Emma in a wide land and, humbly and in tears, bent and kissed the elbow of her sleeve" (116).

But even though Stephen imagines salvation—"Take hands, Stephen and Emma. It is a beautiful evening now in heaven. You have erred but you are always my children" (116)—the retreat is not over. The sermons go on and on, reviewing biblical sins and their punishments: Noah's flood, Adam and Eve eating the forbidden fruit, and Jesus, enduring the torture of crucifixion in order to save those who would obey "the word of His church" while those who "persisted in their wickedness" (119) would be consigned to hell. The relentless cruelty of hell afflicts all the human senses as its suffocating closure makes sinners "not even able to remove from the eye a worm that gnaws it," enveloping them in a stench like that produced by "some foul and putrid corpse that has lain rotting and decomposing in the grave, a jellylike mass of liquid corruption" (120). Sinners in hell are made to feel a fire raging inside and outside the body. "The blood seethes and boils in the veins, the brains are boiling in the skull," the students are told, "the bowels a redhot mass of burning pulp, the tender eyes flaming like molten balls" (121). No wonder Stephen leaves this last sermon with "his legs shaking and the scalp of his head trembling as though it had been touched by ghostly fingers" (124).

Pages and pages of depressing sermons represent a strange narrative maneuver in this chapter because they intrude with a voice that is neither a narrator's nor a description of Stephen's thoughts, becoming sufficiently tedious that readers may long to be simply done with them. But their function is to justify Stephen's extreme emotional reaction in contrast to that of his classmates who are more easily able to shake off the sermons' oppressive effects. His friend Heron, for example, appears to be little affected by the horrendous prose, complaining more about the rain: "I wish it would clear up. I had arranged to go for a spin on the bike with some fellows out by Malahide," he says, while Stephen, sitting at his desk, has been gratefully thinking, "He had not died. God had spared him still" (125). The retreat continues, going on and on, but now guiding the way to repentance and its promise of forgiveness.

Together, these lengthy and unrelenting sermons constitute a climax in the moral crisis of Stephen's adolescence, one that will give him literal nightmares of hell, "That was his hell. God had allowed him to see the hell reserved for his sins: stinking, bestial, malignant" (138), sufficiently terrifying to drive him to confession where he will be obliged to tell all. "His sins trickled from his lips, one by one, trickled in shameful drops from his soul festering and oozing like a sore, a squalid stream of vice" (144). The ugly liquid tropes, already invoked in the sermons, represent the extent to which Stephen has internalized the emotionally evocative prose of the priestly language. The confession is successful as it plucks Stephen from his emotional hell and restores him back to normal life where he will presumably be able to enjoy something as simple as eating breakfast again: "White pudding and eggs and sausages and cups of tea. How simple and beautiful was life after all! And life lay all before him!" (146)

Chapter IV

Religion, however, continues to play an important role in Stephen's life. Clearly, both the terror of the retreat experience and the relief of the confession, will not let Stephen break away from the hold religion has on him now. His daily life is now governed by devotional responsibilities, and we are told that "[e]very part of his day, divided by what he regarded now as the duties of his station in life, circled about its own centre of spiritual energy" (148). The view of this new spiritual life is presented largely through the narrative voice rather than through Stephen's own perceptions, and although its maintenance is difficult, Stephen appears to feel rewarded by it. "Life became a divine gift for every moment and sensation of which, were it even the sight of a single leaf hanging on the twig of a tree, his soul should praise and thank the Giver" (149).

The sermon that once transformed every one of the human senses into a locus of hell now commands Stephen to constrain and discipline his own senses, obliging him to make sight, hearing, smell, taste, and touch instruments of discomfort rather than pleasure, in order to undo his sinful past. This intense self-discipline, however, slowly begins to be challenged by unwelcome intrusions of "insistent voices of the flesh," and "the violence of temptations" (152-3). These temptations are disconcerting to Stephen, to the point where he questions whether he has actually repented completely and sufficiently. "I have amended my life, have I not? he asked himself" (153).

This ends the first section of Chapter IV, and when it resumes, Stephen is in a private, serious, and adult conversation with the Jesuit director of his school, who discusses with him not religion per se, but the conditions and specifics of the priesthood, including such trivial topics as clerical dress. Not surprisingly, this conversation, conducted in a "very different" and ostensibly more mature voice than that normally heard by students, comes to the point when the director asks Stephen "Have you ever felt that you had a vocation?" (157). It seems that Stephen's seriousness and piety, so different from Heron's, have not gone unnoticed by his priestly mentors, for whom they represent the marks of candidacy to the priesthood.

Given the anguished conversation Stephen had undergone after the retreat, the prospect of priesthood may not seem unrealistic. But a few pages earlier it already becomes clear that Stephen has begun thinking of women again, remembering the first time he had felt "beneath his tremulous fingers the brittle texture of a woman's stocking" (155)—a thought he would presumably have banished instantly not long before. It is therefore not surprising that he concedes to the director only that "I have sometimes thought of it" (157). The priest goes on to make a case for the priesthood, as Stephen's thoughts reveal how seriously he has indeed considered this option. But once he parts ways with the priest, he reflects on the "grave and ordered and passionless life" (160) that would await him, and realizes that the "chill and order of the life repelled him" (161). As the narrating voice's description of his thoughts makes clear, Stephen will not become a priest.

But the secular life that awaits Stephen offers no glamor and little hope. He realizes this when he returns to his home with its "latchless" door, and walks down the "naked" hallway to the kitchen, where he sees the "glassjars and jampots which did service for teacups" on the table, along with "a knife with a broken ivory handle" "stuck through the pith of a ravaged turnover" (163). The depressing description of the scene conveys the misery Stephen perceives. And it will get worse, as his brothers and sisters tell him the parents have to move the family once more because the landlord will be putting them out. The children comfort themselves by singing, and Stephen joins them, although he hears in their voices "the recurring note of weariness and pain. All seemed weary of life even before entering upon it," (164), an unpromising beginning of the next phase of his life.

However, the last segment of Chapter IV begins with new hope, as it seems that Stephen may be attending the University. Impatient to learn the outcome of his father's discussion with the tutor, he takes off and heads toward Dublin Bay, passing classmates diving and swimming and calling to him. But his thoughts are elsewhere, caught up finding perfect words to describe the day—"A day of dappled seaborne clouds" (166)—by means of a narrative voice intensely poetic in its description of the way Stephen perceives "the sensible world through the prism of a language manycoloured and richly storied" (167). And as Stephen looks at the cold naked wet bodies of the diving and swimming boys, he hears them call him not only by his first name but also by his "strange" last name, which now takes on for him the mythical significance of Daedalus/Dedalus, "the fabulous artificer" of Greek mythology.

The name now seems to Stephen a prophecy of "the end he had been born to serve," "forging anew in his workshop out of the sluggish matter of the earth a new soaring impalpable imperishable being" (169). Stephen has left behind the promise of one vocation to pursue another. Leaving his classmates, he takes his shoes and socks off and begins wading in a rivulet by the sea, where he sees a girl standing "before him in midstream, alone and still, gazing out to sea. She seemed like one whom magic had changed into the likeness of a strange and beautiful seabird" (171). The narrative voice describes her in simple poetic language, with rhythmic repetitions that mimic the movements as she stirs the water in which she is standing "hither and thither, hither and thither" until Stephen erupts in a cry of ecstasy, "Heavenly God! cried Stephen's soul, in an outburst of profane joy" (171).

His new life has begun, "To live, to err, to fall, to triumph, to recreate life out of life!" (172). He walks along the shore to a nook where he lies down and goes to sleep, waking up to a moonlit evening. The chapter ending appears to offer the lovely beginning of the artist's entry into a new life.

Chapter V

Given the promising tone of the ending of the previous chapter, it is a shock when Chapter V begins in a Dedalus kitchen, one that is more squalid than the last, with watery tea and yellow drippings, pawntickets that Stephen picks up with greasy fingers, a box "speckled with lousemarks," and a "battered alarm clock that was lying on its side" (174). The dramatic contrast between Stephen's inner and outer worlds, the world of his imagination and his material surroundings, has perdured throughout his journey from boyhood at Clongowes to adulthood.

His adulthood is itself questionable when we see Stephen's mother "scrub his neck and root into the folds of his ears and into the interstices at the wings of his nose" (175), as though he were still a child. His father has become coarser over the years, shouting: "Is your lazy bitch of a brother gone out yet?"—an insult to which Stephen responds by focusing on grammar, "He has a curious idea of genders if he thinks a bitch is masculine."

This preoccupation continues after he leaves the house and heads off to the University. "His own consciousness of language was ebbing from his brain and trickling into the very words themselves," the narrative voice tells us, a tendency evident as Stephen makes "wayward rhythms" like the one beginning "*The ivy whines upon the wall*" (179). But his fascination with language has a social dimension as well, and turns out to be a reason for his unlikely friendship with Davin, "the peasant student" (180) whose "rare phrases of Elizabethan English" and "quaintly turned versions of Irish idioms" (195) intrigue Stephen, even as his worship of "the sorrowful legend of Ireland" (181) conflicts him.

Davin tells "Stevie" about an encounter deep in the country with a young pregnant woman alone in her cottage, who invites him to spend the night. The simple poetic narrative is powerfully evocative to Stephen of rural Irish women, "a type of her race and his own, a batlike soul waking to the consciousness of itself in darkness and secrecy and loneliness" (183). Davin is only one of the many figures in the university who conjure up for Stephen the cultural and linguistic complications of Irish social life. While discussing language with the dean of studies, who is trying to light a fire in the classroom, Stephen is distracted from Newman's use of language by the priest's use of the word "funnel" in place of the word "tundish." The priest is English, and Stephen later writes in his journal that he looked up the word "tundish" and found it to be "English and good old blunt English too. Damn the dean of studies and his funnel!" he notes. "What did he come here for to teach us his own language or to learn it from us" (251).

Subtly, Joyce introduces here Stephen's awareness of the political suppression of Ireland's native Gaelic language by the British. About the dean of studies, he thinks: "The language in which we are speaking is his before it is mine" . . . "His language, so familiar and so foreign, will always be for me an acquired speech" (189). Not only this Englishman living in Ireland, but an Irish student from Ulster, draws Stephen's attention to the varieties of language expressions all around him. "Are we likely to be asked questions on applied science?" (193) the student asks, and Stephen notes that he pronounces "the word *science* as a monosyllable" (194).

Stephen's simple poetic ruminations on the sounds and rhythms of words are slowly becoming political, and by the time he encounters his friend Davin again, this point erupts into the whole Gaelic language controversy. "Why don't you learn Irish?" (202) Davin asks him, and when he presses Stephen about this, Stephen replies angrily: "My ancestors threw off their language and took another. . . They allowed a handful of foreigners to subject them. Do you fancy I am going to pay in my own life and person debts they made?" (203). To Davin's rejoinder, he adds, "When the soul of a man is born in this country there are nets flung at it to hold it back from flight. You talk to me of nationality, language, religion. I shall try to fly by those nets." It will be many more pages before Stephen's thoughts reveal that he may already be invoking the mythical figure embedded in his strange Irish name of Dedalus, "the hawklike man whose name he bore soaring out of his captivity on osierwoven wings" (225).

But Stephen's focus at this time of his life is less on politics than on elevating his interest in language and art into the theoretical sphere of aesthetics. He wants to explore the fundamentals of beauty in a logical and rational way, and he does this not only by reading Aristotle ("Aristotle has not defined pity and terror. I have" [204]), as well as Plato and Aquinas, but also by engaging friends and listeners in one-sided dialogues to explore his theories. This strategy of making Stephen's thoughts spoken and shared rather than private and silent energizes his rather complex and arguably pedantic formulations, while also displaying the elegance of his speech.

Stephen's first interlocutor is his friend Lynch, a blunt, down-to-earth fellow with his own flair for verbal play, like substituting the word "yellow" for the vulgar "bloody" in his curses. "Damn your yellow insolence" he responds when Stephen offers him a cigarette, because "I know you are poor" (204). But Lynch it not above intellectual engagement. "What is art? What is the beauty it expresses?" (207) he asks as Stephen launches into an aesthetic discussion that formulates his thoughts into their own formal and often symmetrical language. "Truth is beheld by the intellect which is appeased by the most satisfying relations of the intelligible: beauty is beheld by the imagination which is appeased by the most satisfying relations of the sensible" (208), he explains. This abstraction is amplified when Stephen points "to a basket which a butcher's boy had slung inverted on his head.—Look at that basket, he said" (212). Stephen now goes on to analyze the mental perception of the basket as an aesthetic image through a process that he divides into the categories of *integritas, consonantia, and claritas* borrowed from Thomas Aquinas's *Summa*

Theologica. Lynch, who is familiar with the terms and appears to understand Stephen's points perfectly, keeps the lecture down to earth by responding to his analysis with "Bull's eye!" (212). Stephen ends the discussion by returning to art's effect on the personality of the artist that "finally refines itself out of existence, impersonalises itself, so to speak" (215). In a sense, Stephen's theory of art anticipates some of the characteristics that Joyce's contemporary modernists like T. E. Hulme and Ezra Pound propounded in their preference for Classicism, with its focus on objectivity and impersonality, over emotionally intense Romanticism.

When Stephen and Lynch arrive at the library, Lynch whispers "Your beloved is here" (215). The complicated narrative will make it difficult to figure out what is going on, and we have to assemble the story from different hints here and there. The first one was given earlier when Davin guessed why Stephen dropped out of the Gaelic class. "Is it on account of that certain young lady and Father Moran?" (202). Apparently, Stephen saw Emma talking and laughing with a priest and was overcome with jealousy that has not yet resolved. "She has no priest to flirt with" (216) he thinks bitterly when he sees her at the library, but she nonetheless inspires him to experience what has become referred to as Stephen's *wet dream* that night. "Towards dawn he awoke. O what sweet music! His soul was all dewy wet," and he is described as experiencing "[a]n enchantment of the heart" (217). The enchantment and ecstasy of his dream trigger verses that "passed from his mind to his lips" and that result in the production of a villanelle that he is obliged to write on the rough cardboard surface of an empty cigarette wrapper, the only paper he can find.

The contrast between Stephen's material condition and his poetic exaltation at this moment is epitomized by the narration's description of his writing in a "roselike glow" that "sent forth its rays of rhyme; ways, days, blaze, praise, raise" (218). This entire episode is a curious dramatization of the aesthetic process that Stephen had just systematically and meticulously expounded to Lynch the day before—the process of transforming emotion and feeling into the music and rhythm of language:

> *Are you not weary of ardent ways,*
> *Lure of the fallen seraphim?*
> *Tell no more of enchanted days.* (223)

The poem spreads over six verses, articulating over and over the tension of passion and the anxiety of its fading. As the next section of Chapter V begins, we are given the first indications that Stephen may be planning a departure from his city and his homeland, an enactment of the flight of his mythical ancestor.

The scene begins tellingly with Stephen watching the flight of birds, "a dark flash, a swerve, a flash again, a dart aside, a curve, a flutter of wings" (224), serving as a portent of Dedalus, "the hawklike man whose name he bore soaring out of his captivity on osierwoven wings" (225). He enters the library to find his friend Cranly, and as they leave, they engage in banter with friends on the porch outside, until Emma at some point appears to pass. This triggers another round of complex feelings in Stephen, less ecstatic and more troublesome than before because they contest the poetic inspiration that had inflamed him to write the villanelle. In his imagination, he now "smelt her body," "a wild and languid" smell (233), followed by a moment when a louse crawls over the back of his neck and triggers a vision of his own degraded physical condition. "The life of his body, illclad, illfed, louseeaten, made him close his eyelids in a sudden spasm of despair" (234).

His earlier flight into poetic enchantment has landed him back on an aesthetically and romantically eroded earth. "Well then, let her go and be damned to her. She could love some clean athlete who washed himself every morning to the waist and had black hair on his chest. Let her" (234).

After more banter, Stephen tells Cranly that he needs to speak to him, and they leave to engage in another dialogue. The urgency behind Stephen's need to speak to Cranly has to do not with Emma, but with his mother. "I had an unpleasant quarrel this evening" (238), he begins, and concedes that it was about religion. Religion has been a center of conflict throughout Stephen's narrative—recall the early Christmas dinner scene, his attack by classmates at Belvedere, the scary religious retreat and the nightmares it induced, among others. Stephen's mother merely wants him to make his "easter duty," an obligation to receive Holy Communion during the Easter season, and he has decided he "will not serve." The conversation that ensues is skillful on Cranly's part, asking questions to prompt Stephen to articulate his feelings about the church, about religion and faith, about his mother, his family, and his circumstances in life.

The questions are simple, and so are Stephen's answers. They initially review his biography as we have been reading it, his family's prosperous beginning, the "[n]ine or ten" children that came along, and his father's failure to cultivate and pursue a profession. Cranly takes this information and uses it gently to point out to Stephen what this kind of life has been like for his mother. "Your mother must have gone through a good deal of suffering, he said then. Would you not try to save her from suffering more even if . . . or would you?" (241). "If I could," Stephen replies. This raises more inner conflicts about religion, and the solution is not simple. On the one hand, Stephen cannot be certain whether the communion wafer is or is not the body of Christ, and therefore fears violating the faith by making an insincere communion. But he is also afraid of "the chemical action which would be set up in my soul by a false homage to a symbol behind which are massed twenty centuries of authority and veneration" (243).

By now Stephen and Cranly have moved into an area of villas, trees, and hedges, where they hear a young servant girl sing about sweet *Rosie O'Grady*, whose rhythms Cranly describes as "real poetry": "There's real poetry for you, he said. There's real love" (244). When they resume their discussion, Stephen makes it clear that "Probably I shall go away" (245). The earlier premonition, when he saw the birds and thought of the flight of his namesake Dedalus, appears to have taken hold as a probability for him, and although Cranly tries to assure him that his conflicts with religion should not drive him away—"There are many good believers who think as you do" (245)—Stephen appears to have reached a resolution to his conflicts: "I will not serve that in which I no longer believe whether it call itself my home, my fatherland or my church," he says. "I will try to express myself in some mode of life or art as freely as I can and as wholly as I can, using for my defence the only arms I allow myself to use—silence, exile, and cunning" (246–7).

And so, the final section of *Portrait* begins with Stephen now summarizing in simple written prose the scene we have just been given to witness: "*20 March.* Long talk with Cranly on the subject of my revolt. He had his grand manner on. I supple and suave. Attacked me on the score of love for one's mother. Tried to imagine his mother: cannot" (247).

The contrast between Stephen's own written words and the written narrated words we have been reading is startling, jolting us back into remembering that we have not heard his thoughts as much as external summations of his thoughts. The journal entries revisit the entire last chapter, offering accounts of his interactions with Cranly, Lynch, Dixon, Davin, his mother, his father, the dean of studies. These thoughts are colorful, young, ironic, and playful in style—very different from the sober narrative throughout the work. His description of his last meeting with Emma is engaging, making a little fun of her earnest questions and his less than satisfactory responses, and her polite departure when she "said she hoped I would do what I said. Now I call that friendly, don't you?" (252).

It is difficult for us not to wonder what it might have been like had the whole book been written from this perspective, in this style, although as Stephen's journal nears its end, it begins to merge back into the earlier narrative prose: "Welcome, O life! I go to encounter for the millionth time the reality of experience and to forge in the smithy of my soul the uncreated conscience of my race" (252). And with a final mythic prayer, "Old father, old artificer, stand me now and ever in good stead" (253), *A Portrait of the Artist as a Young Man* comes to an end.

4

Ulysses

Joyce apparently thought of writing a work based on Homer's *Odyssey* as early as 1906 or 1907. Joyce scholar Michael Groden suggests that he might first have thought of producing it as a story, like the ones in *Dubliners*, or as a short book (*'Ulysses' in Progress* 5).

Serious work on *Ulysses* did not begin until 1914 and 1915, however, and its earliest production came in the form of episodes published in the magazine the *Little Review*, whose European editor was Ezra Pound, and in the *Egoist*, edited by Harriet Shaw Weaver. Joyce, who had already encountered censorship issues with the seemingly innocuous stories of *Dubliners*, inevitably incurred them with these early chapters of *Ulysses* as well, and in 1921 Margaret Anderson and Jane Heap, the U.S. editors of the *Little Review*, were convicted of publishing obscenity in the United States in relation to the sexual innuendoes in the book's "Nausicaa" episode. These censorship problems made it clear that the completed *Ulysses* could not reasonably be published in English-speaking countries, and as a result, Sylvia Beach, the owner of a Parisian bookstore called *Shakespeare and Company*, offered to have her business publish *Ulysses* in France. Joyce gratefully accepted.

Beach found a printer in Dijon who managed to send two copies of the printed book to Paris by train on the morning of February 2, 1922, Joyce's 40th birthday. Beach met the train at the station, was handed the copies of *Ulysses* by the conductor, rushed to Joyce's flat in a taxi and gave him his first copy of his book. The other copy she displayed in her bookstore, where people crowded in all day to see it.

Ulysses became a sensation among intellectuals, including Americans who brought it back to their country, spurring publishers like Bennett Cerf of Random House to want to publish it in the U.S. This required another obscenity trial, but over a decade later the social climate in the country had changed sufficiently that *Ulysses* was declared not to be obscene in a famous ruling by Judge John Woolsey in 1933. In spite of its success, *Ulysses* was not immune to criticism, for, in addition to its possible lewdness, readers were also daunted, and occasionally bored, by its length, its difficulty, and the strangeness and inconsistency of its prose. "More than one reviewer compared *Ulysses* to a telephone directory," Joyce critic Joseph Brooker reported ("Reception History," *The Cambridge Companion to 'Ulysses'* 24).

In response to readers' confusion, Joyce eventually created schema delineating aspects of the book for his Italian translator, Carlo Linati, and the French writer Valery Larbaud, that included such critical information as Homeric titles for the episodes, times when they occur, their characters, scene or place, and more evocative aspects such as art, technique, and even colors that might be thought to define the various episodes. Linati received his schema in 1920, before the book's publication, but it has since become indispensable for understanding its relationship to Homer's *Odyssey*, and for giving us the titles by which we now identify the chapters in *Ulysses*. None of this information is given overtly in the book itself, which signals only that it is divided into three sections and 18 chapters, none of which have titles or names. Yet, it is now almost impossible to imagine how one could discuss the work if we could not instantly signal its content without such titles as "Telemachus," "Wandering Rocks," "Circe," or "Penelope."

Given its title, a preliminary discussion of *Ulysses* invariably requires discussion of its relationship to its mythical intertext, Homer's *Odyssey*. This work details the many daunting challenges and obstacles encountered by Odysseus, the king of Ithaca, on his 10-year journey home after the end of the Trojan War.

Odysseus battles monsters and one-eyed giants, becomes detained by enthralled women or lured by Sirens, is obliged to visit the underworld, and struggles with wandering rocks and violent winds at sea. In his absence, his wife Penelope faces her own challenges back home in Ithaca. As the decade goes by, Odysseus is presumed dead and suitors put increasing pressure on Penelope to choose one of them as his successor, prompting her son Telemachus to search for, and eventually find, his lost father and bring him home. Together, father and son return to the palace where Odysseus manages to defeat the suitors in a game devised by Penelope, and kill them. After convincing his wife that he is indeed her husband by revealing that he knows the secret of their marriage bed, built out of a living tree, both the rule of his kingdom and the unity of his family are restored.

In *Ulysses*, it is Stephen Dedalus, previously encountered in *A*

Portrait of the Artist as a Young Man, who takes on the role of Telemachus, struggling as the son of a father who neglects his forsaken children after his wife's death. As we first meet Stephen, he is living in the Martello Tower with a roommate and visitor. On this morning he embarks on a journey to earn a living, to establish a reputation as a writer and poet, and to come to terms with guilt because he refused to pray at his mother's deathbed. He is not consciously aware that he is searching for a father, but in the fourth chapter of *Ulysses* we encounter his Odysseus (or Ulysses)—a Jewish man named Leopold Bloom who is in the opposite situation. Having lost a newborn son 11 years before, he subconsciously longs for a son.

In the course of his day in Dublin, Bloom has experiences mirroring those of Odysseus. He attends a funeral where he encounters the dead as Odysseus does in Hades, and he experiences metaphoric squalls and winds while visiting the newspaper office where he works as an advertising canvasser. Later in the day, he is erotically excited by a young woman lifting her skirts on the beach, and encounters a drunken bigot in a bar whose one-sided view of nationality and race reminds us of the *Odyssey's* one-eyed Cyclops. Eventually he encounters Stephen Dedalus, his Telemachus, in the lounge of a maternity hospital, and follows him on a sojourn to the red-light district of Dublin. There, Bloom is transformed into a metaphorical animal of sorts when his encounter with the brothel's Madam stimulates masochistic fantasies—a transformation evocative of Homer's Circe who turns men into swine. When Stephen gets into a fight with a soldier there, Bloom takes him to his house where they drink a cup of cocoa and appear to find some peace before Stephen goes off into the night.

What about those suitors Odysseus has to fight and kill on his return to Ithaca? It turns out that the loss of the infant son has interfered with the Blooms' sex life, leaving his wife Molly with little sexual satisfaction, and prompting her to begin an affair with the man who will be taking her on a concert tour. After Bloom gets into bed and goes to sleep, his Penelope will sort through her own complex feelings about her husband and her new lover, and slay the suitor, as it were, in her own way by going to sleep with highly romantic and loving memories of Leopold.

These are the Odyssean contours of *Ulysses,* although one important difference between the works must be noted. While the *Odyssey* encompasses a period of 10 years and covers a large geographical territory, *Ulysses* takes place on a single day—June 16,

1904—spent by the characters entirely in the city of Dublin. This is another example of Joyce's Classicism, as he adopts the structural principle of unity of time, place, and action mandated by classical literary construction.

Book I

1. Telemachus

I will now explore the three books of *Ulysses* in some detail. Each one is of different length, with Book I encompassing only three chapters, Book II covering 12 chapters, and Book III, three. The middle section of my discussion will therefore be much longer than the others.

The first chapter of Book I is titled "Telemachus," and introduces us to Stephen Dedalus on the morning of the day in question, Thursday, June 16, 1904. We meet him at what will turn out to be the flat top of a seaside tower whose "gunrest" indicates that it is a fortress built by the British to protect the Irish coast from a French invasion during the 19th century French Revolutionary wars. It is morning and a young fellow named Malachi ("Buck") Mulligan is shaving and making allusions to the Catholic mass. Stephen is described as "displeased and sleepy" (*Ulysses* 3), a situation caused by a nightmare triggered by the British visitor named Haines, whose "guncase" made Stephen extremely nervous, and presumably caused him to lose sleep: "Out here in the dark with a man I don't know raving and moaning to himself about shooting a black panther" (4).

The presence of Haines will not be Stephen's only source of conflict with his roommate, however. As Mulligan looks at the sea and tropes it as a "mother," he blurts out "The aunt thinks you killed your mother," (5) triggering Stephen's own worst guilt over the possible impact of his refusal to pray at her deathbed. Three conflicts have been laid out here in just the first pages of the work: Stephen's conflict over, and later with, Haines; his conflict with Mulligan's insensitive nature; and his conflict with religion which produced a familial conflict with his mother.

Stephen's conflict with Haines does not erupt until after breakfast when Haines begins to ask Stephen about his faith, and Stephen responds that he is a servant of two masters, "an English and an Italian," that is, the "Roman catholic and apostolic church," and the "imperial British state" (17). Presumably, Stephen refers obliquely to the ironic situation that allows the British Oxford student to study and speak

Gaelic, while Irish men and women like Stephen and the milk-woman who brings them their morning milk ("I'm ashamed I don't speak the language myself. I'm told it's a grand language by them that knows" [13]) have been historically deprived of their native tongue by British rule. This situation has implications for Stephen's ambitions as an artist because it will oblige him to write in English, his conqueror's language.

2. Nestor

The political situation confronting young Irishmen like Stephen will emerge again in the next chapter when he goes off to his day job as a teacher in a private school for boys in Dalkey. This second chapter is titled "Nestor" in reference to Telemachus's journey, which leads him to visit the "master charioteer" Nestor on the Greek mainland in search of his father. Stephen first teaches his class ancient history and then goes on to the topic of literature, which on this morning focuses on John Milton's elegy "Lycidas."

Neither history nor literature taught at this Irish school addresses anything pertaining to Ireland on this day. Stephen helps a student who had to rework an assignment, and then is called to the study of the headmaster Mr. Deasy to receive his pay. Like the Homeric Nestor, Mr. Deasy tries to function as a mentor or surrogate father to Stephen, giving him advice about saving money, something his biological father has certainly failed to do. But the discussion is full of hidden conflict with little benefit to Stephen. Mr. Deasy is clearly pro-British, and his citation of "the proudest word you will ever hear from an Englishman's mouth" is highly ironic: "I paid my way" (25). It does prompt Stephen to enumerate his own copious debts in his mind, but of course England at that time exploited numerous colonies throughout the world to pay its way.

As Deasy goes on to promote the politics of Irish Protestantism and chides Stephen by saying "You fenians forget some things," Stephen silently recounts historical moments of oppression that counter Deasy's claims: "The lodge of Diamond in Armagh the splendid behung with corpses of papishes. Hoarse, masked and armed, the planters' covenant" (26). We see here the important role that Joyce's use of "stream of consciousness" or "interior monologue" plays at a moment like this in *Ulysses*, because while Stephen cannot openly argue with the headmaster, he is free to think what he likes, and we are given his resistance and opposition by being privy to his thoughts.

Mr. Deasy clearly serves as neither a worthy mentor nor an inspiring father figure for Stephen, although his most insulting slur will point prophetically in the direction in which he will find such a model. After typing a letter on hoof and mouth disease in cattle that he asks Stephen to deliver to local newspapers, Deasy runs after Stephen to impart a last political axiom. "Ireland, they say, has the honour of being the only country which never persecuted the jews. Do you know that? No. And do you know why?" Deasy's answer is: "Because she never let them in" (30).

What began as a possibly humane historical observation has turned out to be a nasty joke that cracks Deasy up, making him laugh so hard that he coughs up phlegm. Fortunately, the joke's premise is not true, because the Irish did take in a reasonably sizeable Jewish population, and it is in that particular pool that the novel's Telemachus will find a worthy father figure for Stephen in the person of the Jewish Leopold Bloom.

3. Proteus

The third chapter of Book I, called "Proteus" after a shape-shifting figure in the *Odyssey*, begins with a line that must come from Stephen's thoughts, and thereby puts the technique of "stream of consciousness" or "interior monologue" at the forefront of the chapter. "Ineluctable modality of the visible: at least that if no more, thought through my eyes" (31). Only the "my" indicates that this is not a third person narration, and the thoughts that follow make it clear that this is not a conversation but an interior rumination.

The third-person voice does enter in the next paragraph to identify the thinker as Stephen, and so we are launched into a chapter with effectively no dialogue, as Stephen walks alone along Sandymount strand, thinking about this and that, watching two cockle-pickers and their dog approach, and, at one point, sitting down to write a brief poem on a scrap of paper torn from Mr. Deasy's letter. How does Joyce manage to make an entire chapter grounded in just the thoughts of a single person with few actions and events (many of them trivial, like Stephen picking his nose or urinating) interesting? The answer is in the variety of topics and issues Stephen contemplates, and in the diversity of styles his thoughts assume as he entertains them. As he thinks about the problem of vision, and the "modality of the visible," he will open and close his eyes as he walks. When he sees two women coming down to the beach, he invents names, addresses, and occupations for them.

He recounts memories of visits to his uncle's home, complete with lively conversations, and pokes fun at himself for his youthful pretensions, which have all come to naught. "Cousin Stephen, you will never be a saint. Isle of saints. You were awfully holy, weren't you?" (34), the narrative tells us as his consciousness engages in conversation with himself. He had thought of visiting his aunt Sara, but passes the house and goes on, remembering his time in Paris and his friendship with a fellow named Kevin Egan, recalling Egan's words, "I was a strapping young gossoon at that time, I tell you. I'll show you my likeness one day" (36). The bloated carcass of a dog on the sand attracts a lively dog who comes bounding toward him, and here we see the narrative's prose turn protean, using tropes to produce shape-shifting images of the dog as bounding like a "hare," trotting its "shanks" with its "forehoofs," panting with a "wolf's tongue," and loping off at a "calf's gallop" (38-9). The dog has been transformed into many animals, suitable for the name by which its owner calls him, "Tatters! Outofthat, you mongrel!" (39).

While remembering a dream he had of being on a "[s]treet of harlots"(39), and thinking of women, Stephen begins to compose a poem that, while perhaps not following the tradition of the Irish writer Bram Stoker, conjures up a vampire. "He comes, pale vampire, through storm his eyes, his bat sails bloodying the sea, mouth to her mouth's kiss" (40). Thinking of his own teeth, he wonders if he should use the money he just earned to see a dentist, and the chapter ends, as he looks over his shoulder, to see "a silent ship" (42).

Book II

4. Calypso

The fourth chapter of *Ulysses*, the first of Book II, begins with a name we have not encountered before: "Mr Leopold Bloom" (45). The three young men in Book I were never referred to as Mr Dedalus, or Mr Haines, so we can infer that this gentleman belongs to the category of Mr Deasy, although the first thing we learn about him is not his occupation but his appetite and taste for food, "Mr Leopold Bloom ate with relish the inner organs of beasts and fowls." The narration takes us right into his gut, as it were, and this will be true in more ways than one as the chapter develops.

The setting is a kitchen, where he is preparing breakfast, which explains why he may be thinking of food and why the narration gives us a preview of his upcoming trip to the butcher store to buy a pork kidney. But first, he prepares a tray with bread and butter and tea that he takes upstairs to the bedside of a woman we infer is his wife. The theme of breakfast suggests that this chapter has moved back in time to the beginning of the first chapter and its breakfast scene in the Martello Tower.

But Mr. Bloom's milieu is far more intensely domestic, feeding his cat milk in his kitchen, visiting the butcher shop, picking up the mail from inside his door when he returns, reading it, chatting with his wife, and after breakfast is over, going to the outhouse for his postprandial bowel movement. We are given much greater intimacy here with a literary figure than we have been given in Victorian or even other early modernist novels, suggesting that Joyce was interested in breaking ground not only in the area of style and writing, but also in representation and depiction.

In just one chapter, a rich portrait of Bloom develops. We will not learn that he is Jewish until later, although we receive a veiled hint in an awkward moment in the butcher shop when the Jewish Dlugacz appears to want to talk to Bloom about something and he balks, thinking "No: better not: another time" (49). The mail he picks up when he returns home includes a letter addressed to "Mrs Marion Bloom," presumably his wife, since he takes it up to the woman in the bedroom. There is also a card and a letter that turns out to be from "Milly." The Blooms have a 15-year-old daughter, we learn, who celebrated her birthday the day before, and who is living in the town of Mullingar where she is training as a photographer's apprentice. As Bloom reads her letter thanking him for the birthday gift he sent her, his thoughts reveal an early family tragedy that will recur to haunt him all day.

Remembering the midwife who helped deliver Milly, he thinks "She knew from the first poor little Rudy wouldn't live. " The Blooms have lost a son shortly after his birth: "He would be eleven now if he had lived" (54). It will be some time before we figure out how this information relates to the *Odyssey*, where it is, after all, the son who worries that he has lost his father and not the father who has lost his son. But although the situations of Stephen and Bloom may be reversed, they are reminiscent of Homer as the novel progresses, with Stephen's Telemachus needing a father, even if he doesn't search for him actively, and Bloom's Odysseus needing a son and behaving very much like a father when he finds a surrogate in Stephen that evening.

But the father-son relationship is not the only Odyssean theme introduced in this chapter. There is the letter to "Mrs Marion Bloom"—not "Mrs Leopold Bloom" we should note—that the woman in bed tucks under her pillow after she reads it and does not share with her husband. Bloom is clearly a bit disconcerted by it—"Bold hand. Marion" (52)—and asks her "Who was the letter from?" It turns out that his wife is a singer, and the letter is a note from her impresario making an appointment to bring the program for an upcoming concert tour he has arranged for her. His name is "Boylan," and we may here be alerted that if Bloom's wife Molly is the analog of the Homeric Penelope, then this Boylan may be the suitor threatening the husband's place in his palace and in the life of his wife. And, so, two major themes from the *Odyssey*—the father and son separation and the wife's approach by suitors or a suitor—have been introduced in this first chapter of Book II.

5. Lotus Eaters

Most of the *Odyssey* describes the varied and startling adventures of Odysseus during his 10-year journey home to Ithaca after the ending of the Trojan War. Leopold Bloom's own odyssey, as it were, is compacted into a single day.

He leaves his home after breakfast and visit to the outhouse, and spends the rest of the day in Dublin, encountering his own varied adventures along the way. It begins innocuously enough in the next chapter, with a stop at the post office, where he picks up a letter addressed, curiously, to a "Henry Flower Esq" (59). He then stops at a church where Mass is being said, drops by the chemist's to order some lotion for his wife and pick up a bar of soap, before he heads to the Turkish baths. The Homeric parallel gives the chapter the title "Lotus-Eaters" in reference to a visit Odysseus and his men make to an island where the friendly inhabitants offer them lotus-blossoms to eat, which make the men drowsy and forgetful. This chapter focuses on Leopold Bloom's passivity, his attendance at a religious service Karl Marx might have considered an "opiate," his visit to a chemist whose fragrant lotions might remind us of the palliative lotus-blossoms, and that mysterious letter to a man named "Flower."

Why is Bloom getting a letter at a post office, when he has just had mail delivered to his home? The letter turns out to be from a woman named Martha who tries to mimic the pornographic chiding of a brothel Madam who calls him a "naughty boy" and tells him "I am awfully angry with you. I do wish I could punish you for that" (63). If his wife Molly entertains a suitor, Bloom has apparently initiated his own epistolary affair of sorts with a woman he has never met, and to whom he sends stamps and money to encourage provocative missives that appeal to his masochistic fantasies.

These initial signals of infidelity on both parts suggest that there is something wrong with the Bloom marriage, although we begin to learn what it is only in the next chapter, "Hades," when Bloom is in a carriage with Stephen's father and another friend to attend a funeral. Hearing Simon Dedalus talk about his son Stephen makes Bloom feel envious and think regretfully about his own lost son, "If little Rudy had lived" (73). But now we learn something quite startling. According to Bloom, little Rudy was conceived when Molly looked out the window one morning and saw two dogs copulating, a sight that sexually aroused her to want to make love with her husband—"Give us a touch, Poldy. God, I'm dying for it. How life begins" (74). It is not until a later chapter that the final piece of the puzzle falls into place, when Bloom thinks about sex with his wife Molly and admits "Could never like it again after Rudy" (137). He appears to blame a sex act stimulated by animalistic lust for the death of little Rudy, as well as the subsequent impairment of his sex life with Molly. Unlike Odysseus and Penelope, who are separated geographically for a decade, the Blooms are separated emotionally and sexually over the past 11 years—a tragedy rendered triangular by the loss of their son. Looking ahead, this suggests that if Bloom could have a son restored, he might also be able to restore his physical relationship with his wife.

6. Hades

The death of his son is not Bloom's only loss, as we learn in the chapter titled "Hades," whose Odyssean analogue is the Homeric hero's journey into the underworld, where he encounters the souls of the dead.

But before proceeding to "Hades," we must return to a moment at the end of "Lotus Eaters" that appears utterly insignificant but will turn out to produce a disastrous consequence for Bloom later in the novel. Bloom runs into a fellow named Bantam Lyons who wants to borrow Bloom's newspaper so that he can check the horses that are running in the Gold Cup race on this day. Bloom hands him the paper and tells him he can keep it because "I was just going to throw it away" (70). Unbeknownst to Bloom, one of the horses running in that race is named "Throwaway," and Lyons therefore assumes that Bloom has just given him a veiled tip to bet on a dark horse. Much later in the novel, this will get Bloom into trouble because "Throwaway" will actually win the race, and Bloom will be suspected of having won a huge amount of money and yet not offer to buy drinks for men in a pub, or otherwise share his winnings. It is all a mistake, of course, since Bloom knows nothing about the race or the horse, and never placed a bet. But the silly mistake will nonetheless get him into trouble in a later chapter.

Bloom's encounter with the dead in "Hades" involves not only his thoughts about his dead son, but also a revelation about his father. In this chapter, Bloom rides in a carriage with two friends on their way to attend the funeral of their drunkard friend Paddy Dignam. Bloom hears his friends contemptuously discussing suicide—"They say a man who does it is a coward" (79)—a conversation that reminds him of the suicide of his father after being widowed. Bloom's memory is vividly presented in the style of stream of consciousness that lets the narration enter into his thoughts in the same way it let us into Stephen's in the first three chapters. Bloom remembers the "coroner's sunlit ears, big and hairy," and how the officials thought that his father "was asleep first. Then saw like yellow streaks on his face. Had slipped down to the foot of the bed. Verdict: overdose. Death by misadventure" (80).

The ride to the cemetery also triggers another uncomfortable moment for Bloom when the men doff their hats to a gentleman on the road—his wife's concert organizer "Blazes Boylan" (76), who will be visiting Molly that afternoon. We now hear more overt jealousy in Bloom's thoughts as he wonders: "Is there anything more in him that they she sees? Fascination. Worst man in Dublin." His friends clearly know about Boylan's work with Bloom's wife and so ask him how the concert tour is getting on, an uncomfortable subject for him.

The chapter ends with an even more uncomfortable moment when Bloom is snubbed by a man who once danced with his wife before they were married and who wonders, "what did she marry a coon like that for?" (88)—a comment thankfully not heard by Bloom.

7. *Aeolus*

The next chapter, "Aeolus," opens with a startling departure not only from the book's first six chapters, but also from the novel-writing style at that particular time. A series of capitalized titles separate the paragraphs of the chapter. Once we realize that it is set in a newspaper office, we construe these titles to function like newspaper headlines—a kind of imitative form, as we might think of it. Joyce scholar Karen Lawrence notes that "In 'Aeolus,' the book begins to advertise its own artifice, and in doing so, it calls attention to the processes of reading and writing" (*The Odyssey of Style in 'Ulysses'* 58).

The reader's attention is partly drawn away from the story and the characters and diverted to the style and construction of the chapter. As it happens, the narration of the paragraphs remains relatively normal, and we now see Bloom in his job as an advertising canvasser. He gets paid for getting businesses to buy ads in the newspaper called *The Freeman's Journal*, a job that requires him to negotiate with clients and editors about fees and conditions. A number of men gather in the newspaper office on this day, entering and leaving, and discussing a variety of issues, including the merits of writing styles and famous speeches. In the process, they discuss and produce what might colloquially be termed "hot air"—bluster or emotionally or stylistically exaggerated speech.

There is reference here to the chapter's Homeric title. Aeolus, the keeper of the winds in Greek legend, offers to help Odysseus with his journey by confining violent winds in a bag that Odysseus's men open, thinking there might be treasure inside, and thereby release them. In the chapter, Bloom inadvertently unleashes something of this sort by annoying the editor Miles Crawford when he tries to negotiate a better deal for his client. "Will you tell him he can kiss my arse," Crawford tells Bloom, who thinks to himself, "A bit nervy. Look out for squalls" (120).

Stephen Dedalus turns up at the newspaper office with the letter Mr. Deasy asked him to deliver, and himself delivers to the men a story about two middle-aged Dublin spinsters that the narrative glosses as "Dubliners" (119)—the title of Joyce's own book of short stories. On the level of plot, we see here a curious reversal of estimations of Dubliners by Dubliners—with Stephen honored and respected, while Bloom is ignored and brushed aside. We do not yet see that the slights Bloom receives here may be sparked by anti-Semitism, but we do notice that the wise, witty, and gentle soul he exhibits in his interior monologues is not as respected by his community as we would expect.

8. Lestrygonians

We encounter a similar dynamic in the next chapter, "Lestrygonians," named after a race of cannibals in the *Odyssey*. It is lunchtime, and so the chapter is focused on food and hunger, with Bloom worried about a girl he recognizes as Stephen's skinny sister. "Underfed she looks," Bloom thinks, speculating that she probably lives on "[p]otatoes and marge," and may suffer from malnutrition as she gets older: "Undermines the constitution" (125). He also buys cakes to feed some hungry gulls, and listens sympathetically to his friend Josie Breen, whose chipped handbag and dowdy hat betray poverty brought on by a dysfunctional husband.

When Bloom gets his own modest lunch consisting of a gorgonzola sandwich and a glass of burgundy in Davy Byrnes's pub, he runs into Nosey Flynn, who will later disparage Bloom for presumably supplementing his income by belonging to the Masons. This chapter mirrors Stephen's "Proteus" episode with its predominant focus on Bloom's interior thoughts, and it is here that we get the first full revelation of his affection for and appreciation of his wife. He particularly remembers a highly romantic moment before their marriage, when he and Molly reclined on a bank on Howth Head, a hill north of Dublin overlooking the sea, and shared a kiss. "Ravished over her I lay, full lips full open, kissed her mouth. Yum. Softly she gave me in my mouth the seedcake warm and chewed. Mawkish pulp her mouth had mumbled sweetsour of her spittle. Joy: I ate it: joy" (144).

This memory describes a moment of emotional communion, when food signifying love and sharing is exchanged, producing the opposite of the hunger and need that, elsewhere in the chapter, appears to afflict Bloom's fellow Dubliners.

9. Scylla and Charybdis

The next chapter, "Scylla and Charybdis," turns sharply away from the previous ones to return to Stephen Dedalus, whom we last encountered in the newspaper office. Stephen is now in the National Library of Ireland, where he engages with four Irish intellectuals and writers on the subject of Shakespeare. We construe that Stephen might have come there initially to ask the writer George Russell to deliver a copy of Mr. Deasy's letter to the editor of *The Irish Homestead*, but that he stays to deliver his theories in the hope of impressing the rather distinguished group of gentlemen he finds assembled there.

A startling feature of this chapter is that the names of the literary figures identify them as actual historical personages, rather than imagined characters. Such earlier figures as Mulligan and Haines also have historical prototypes: Joyce's contemporary, the poet and politician Oliver St. John Gogarty and a fellow named Samuel Chenevix Trench, but they are given fictional names. The rather distinguished figure of George Russell, an Irish writer, editor, and poet who published under the name of AE, is presented in his own name and pseudonym, with his historical attributes intact. This is also true of John Eglinton, the pseudonym of William Kirkpatrick Magee, Richard

Irvine Best and Thomas William Lyster, men who also worked as essayists, editors, and translators on the Irish literary scene in 1904.

Joyce's evocation of these figures treats them respectfully and does not dishonor them, but their presence adds a poignancy to Stephen's disappointing failure in the most climactic moment of his day, when—by offering a brilliant lecture—he will try to establish himself as a young intellectual worthy of attention and patronage. This failure is foreshadowed by the significance of the episode's Homeric title, which refers to two extremely dangerous hazards Odysseus must encounter and negotiate in the *Odyssey*: Scylla, a six-headed monster who consumes men, and Charybdis, a whirling maelstrom that sucks ships into a watery abyss.

Stephen will presumably also be caught between a rock and a hard place, as it were, in this particular social and intellectual adventure. Given that his interlocutors have interest in and commitments to the Irish Revival, a lecture on the British literary hero Shakespeare could prove to be controversial. Stephen deals with this by bringing the iconic figure—a man who named Hamlet after his own son Hamnet—down to earth, showing him walking along the river too preoccupied with his play to feed the swans. This draws an immediate objection from George Russell, who dislikes this "prying into the family life of a great man," and objects to this "[p]eeping and prying into greenroom gossip of the day, the poet's drinking, the poet's debts. We have *King Lear*: and it is immortal" (155).

Russell's position on Shakespeare is at odds with Stephen's approach, which is why he may decide to leave early. Before Russell goes, the men begin to discuss a soiree to be held that evening at the home of George Moore, an event to which a few bright young men, including Mulligan and Haines, have been invited. Stephen is obliged to sit there and listen to a discussion about an event in which he has clearly not been included, in spite of the erudition and sophistication of his lecture—a moment that makes him feel like Shakespeare's Cordelia, the slighted daughter of King Lear. Nor has he been asked to submit a poem to a book of "our younger poets' verses" (158) that George Russell is preparing to publish and for which Stephen may have penned his vampire poem earlier in the day.

Yet, Stephen persists with his Shakespeare thesis after Russell leaves, even discussing the bard's financial dealings in less than admirable terms that come close to accusing him of usury. "He drew Shylock out of his own long pocket. The son of a maltjobber and moneylender he was himself a cornjobber and moneylender, with ten tods of corn hoarded in the famine riots" (168). The jab may be a veiled allusion to the callousness of which the British were accused of offering inadequate help to the Irish during the Great Famine caused by a potato blight in the 19th century. Stephen's lecture is given respectful attention, but when it is finished Eglinton asks Stephen if he believes in his own theory, and Stephen incongruously says "No" (175). In response, Eglinton tells him that he should not expect to be paid for publishing it. "You are the only contributor to *Dana* who asks for pieces of silver. Then I don't know about the next number. Fred Ryan wants space for an article on economics" (176).

Not only has Stephen's lecture not impressed Eglinton, but he may even lose what little he earns from his modest publications. His gambit, to solidify and improve his career as an Irish intellectual and literary figure has failed miserably, and Stephen's day—as he leaves the library with a jesting and jibing Mulligan, who arrived there near the end—has lost whatever promise it held.

10. Wandering Rocks

In the *Odyssey*, Odysseus chooses to pass between Scylla and Charybdis rather than navigate the "Wandering Rocks," moving stones in the sea that can pop up anywhere at any time to wreck the ships that venture into their territory. In *Ulysses*, this feature is enacted not thematically but structurally, by having the chapter present an array of scenes that play out at roughly the same time, but in different places throughout the city of Dublin, peopled by a host of different characters. As a result, the episode shows us not only Stephen stopping at a book cart, but also his sisters coming home starving and finding only charity soup donated by a nun for their midday meal.

Bloom also stops to look and drool over dirty books outside a bookshop, and we see its owner coughing and spitting phlegm on the sidewalk. Blazes Boylan orders a fruit basket in a flower shop, but we also see his secretary, Miss Dunne, in his office reading a mystery novel. There is little Patrick Dignam, the son of the man whose funeral Bloom attended that morning, carrying a pork steak home to his now widowed mother. The Reverend John Conmee, the dean at Clongowes, the school Stephen attended when he was a little boy, is on an errand to try to get young the young Dignam lad into a Christian Brothers school. We encounter dozens of characters we have not seen before, like a one-legged British sailor begging for alms, to whom Molly Bloom tosses a coin from her window, and an Italian named Almidano Artifoni, who tries to convince Stephen, in Italian, to pursue a career as a singer rather than a writer.

Dublin is abuzz with people out doing their assorted errands, and as scholar Terence Killeen points out, the chapter does something not seen before. It extends the "stream of consciousness" technique beyond Stephen and Bloom to let us into the thoughts of minor characters so we can see how, and what, they think (*'Ulysses' Unbound* 111). It is little Patrick Dignam, however, whose thoughts give us the sharpest insight into both his sentiments and his style of expression, finding it "blooming dull" to have to sit in the parlor listening to the adults bemoaning the loss of his father, "eating crumbs of the cottage fruitcake, jawing the whole blooming time and sighing" (206).

Joyce ends the chapter with an event that catches almost everyone's attention when a cavalcade leaves the Viceregal Lodge and Phoenix Park and travels throughout the city. The viewers include persons we have yet to meet, like Gerty MacDowell, who admires the aristocratic personages on board in the romantic style of the later "Nausicaa" chapter, as well as Miss Kennedy and Miss Douce of the Ormond hotel, whom we meet immediately in the next chapter, "Sirens."

11. Sirens

In the *Odyssey*, the Sirens are dangerous female figures whose beautiful songs lure sailors to their island, causing shipwrecks on the way. In consequence, music plays a major role in this chapter—not only thematically, but also stylistically. Many critics consider this the chapter where style moves to the forefront in a highly dramatic fashion.

The scene is set in the Ormond bar and hotel, where Miss Kennedy and Miss Douce work as barmaids. Bloom sees Blazes Boylan enter close to the time of his four o'clock appointment with Molly at his home, and he therefore follows him unobtrusively and settles into an adjacent room for dinner. Simon Dedalus is there too, and together with friends Ben Dollard and Father Cowley, he sings to music played on the piano, reversing the gender of the singing Sirens. Boylan meets Lenehan, who prods the barmaids into flirtatious behavior, and after a drink departs in a "jingle" or two-wheeled horse-drawn carriage, to go on to his tryst at the Bloom home. Bloom, who is joined at his meal by Richie Goulding, not only listens to Simon Dedalus sing an aria from Friedrich von Flotow's opera *Martha*, but also writes a letter in response to his own epistolary romantic partner, Martha.

Music and romance abound in this chapter, with Boylan off to see Molly, Bloom writing to Martha, and songs performed throughout the episode. Yet, all this will be subordinated to the musicality of the chapter's style. It begins with a literary version of an overture, which introduces the various figures in the chapter in words that endow them with a musical motif. Bloom, who is sad at the prospect of Boylan visiting Molly, is introduced by "A husky fifenote blew. Blew. Blue Bloom is on the" (210). Boylan, who is happy to be going off in his jingle to visit Bloom's wife, is conjured up as "Jingle jingle jaunted jingling." Even after the overture, musicality infects the prose. Miss Kennedy is described as "Sauntering sadly, gold no more, she twisted twined a hair" (212). Words beginning with "s" and with "tw" are repeated, and "gold no more," repeats the sound of "o" three times, letting the prose sing through the sound of words.

Joyce's love of music is glossed with a reference to his early book of poems titled "Chamber music" (232), whose rhythms and sounds are indeed musical in their evocations. At some point in the chapter we are given the sound of a "Tap" (231). The sound will be repeated at intervals throughout the remainder of the chapter, slowly intensifying to "Tap. Tap" (234), "Tap. Tap. Tap. Tap" (236), "Tap. Tap. Tap. Tap. Tap. Tap. Tap. Tap" (237), until we finally learn where it is coming from. A blind piano tuner has tuned the piano earlier, but left his tuning fork behind and now returns to retrieve it, arriving with "a tapping cane," "taptaptapping" (237). Music is not sentimentalized in this chapter, and to underline this point it ends with the finale of a grand fart, "Pprrpffrrppffff" (239), produced by Bloom's drinking of the burgundy, he supposes.

12. Cyclops

The surprise of the next chapter is that it begins with a first-person narrative voice that we do not recognize. "I was just passing the time of day with old Troy of the D.M.P. at the corner of Arbour hill there and be damned but a bloody sweep came along and he near drove his gear into my eye" (240).

Neither Stephen nor Bloom would produce prose like this in conversation, so who is speaking here? We will never learn the name of the narrator, often referred to as the "nameless one," or "Noman," although we do learn that he is a bill collector or dun, and I will therefore refer to him as the "dun." That opening sentence also points us to the Homeric analog and title of the chapter, because its mention of the danger of having one's eye poked out with a stick refers to the "Cyclops" in the *Odyssey*—a race of cannibalistic one-eyed giants. Odysseus and his men take refuge in a cave that turns out to belong to the Cyclops Polyphemus, who promptly devours two of the men, imprisoning the rest of the crew in his cave to serve as his supper on the next day. When he returns, Odysseus plies the giant with wine until he is drunk, and then pokes out his eye with a sharpened and burnt stick, which allows him and his men to escape the next morning.

The Cyclops in Joyce's chapter is not the narrating dun but a fellow he encounters in Barney Kiernan's bar, who is described in outsized third-person prose as a gigantic figure, "broadshouldered deepchested stronglimbed," "widemouthed largenosed longheaded" (243), who is addressed as "the citizen." The citizen's rampant nationalism allows us to construe him as seeing things from a one-sided perspective, of being one-eyed or prejudiced, as it were, and therefore identifying him as a Cyclops.

The chapter will turn out to be a climactic one for Bloom, who arrives a bit later looking for Martin Cunningham, with whom he plans to help the widowed Mrs. Dignam retrieve some funds from her husband's mortgaged life insurance policy. Bloom is not interested in joining the men in standing rounds of drinks, and therefore opts for a cigar instead—an allusion to Odysseus's burning stick, perhaps. But the gesture also irritates the drinkers, who now begin to think of Bloom as a stingy Jew, an impression that becomes wildly exaggerated when Lenehan turns up.

Lenehan learned earlier in the day that Bloom had supposedly given Bantam Lyons a tip on the Gold Cup winner "Throwaway," and he therefore assumes that when Bloom goes out to look for Martin Cunningham, he has gone to collect his huge winnings, which he keeps secret in order not to share them with rounds of drinks. In a later conversation about nationalism and persecution, Bloom, inveighing against the perpetuation of "national hatred among nations" (271), is bluntly asked to name his nation. The question startles him and he answers "Ireland." "I was born here. Ireland" (272). But he knows what they are driving at, and so owns his Jewish identity as well. "And I belong to a race too, says Bloom, that is hated and persecuted" (273).

When Bloom goes out to look for Martin Cunningham, Lenehan tells the men that Bloom is actually going out to collect his winnings, "He had a few bob on *Throwaway* and he's gone to gather in the shekels" (274). The "shekels" allude to Bloom's Jewishness, and we see the men's anti-Semitism slowly flaring against Bloom: "Mean bloody scut. Stand us a drink itself. Devil a sweet fear! There's a jew for you. All for number one" (279).

By the time Bloom returns to the pub, Martin Cunningham realizes he needs to get him out of there speedily, and as they hastily depart, the citizen hurls an empty biscuit tin at Bloom. He responds to the attack with a vigorous defense of himself and his race: "Mendelssohn was a jew and Karl Marx and Mercadante and Spinoza. And the Saviour was a jew and his father was a jew. Your God" (280).

13. Nausicaa

The possible consequences of this scene are never realized in *Ulysses*, but we can speculate that they might be dire, because the dun does not just narrate what happened at Barney Kiernan's that evening, but presumably also tells this story in another pub on a later occasion. If so, then the people who hear it may believe it as it is told, with the implication that Bloom did indeed win big, and refused to divulge or share his winnings. This could change Bloom's reputation in Dublin from that of a generous fellow to a stingy one, making him a victim of more anti-Semitic slander in the future.

At the time of the story, however, Bloom gets a brief respite by walking to the strand to watch three young women and three little children, including two little boys who build sandcastles and play ball. This is the "Nausicaa" episode whose Odyssean counterpart has Odysseus, alone and naked, washed up on a shore where the Princess Nausicaa and her maids discover him while washing laundry.

Although it is narrated in the third-person, the first part of this chapter represents the perspective of one of the young women on the beach, Gerty MacDowell, who is there with her friends Cissy Caffrey and Edy Boardman. Gerty appears to have a romantic disposition inspired by romance novels and other popular literature, and the prose depicting her echoes that spirit: "The waxen pallor of her face was almost spiritual in its ivorylike purity though her rosebud mouth was a genuine Cupid's bow, Greekly perfect" (286). Gerty certainly does not speak like this, but perhaps wishes that she could, like Maria in "Clay" who also is also described as she might wish to be represented, rather than as she could or would be able to describe herself.

As the twin boys, Tommy and Jacky Caffrey, play ball, attended by the three young women, Bloom is watching them. Gerty, aware of Bloom's presence, gradually turns her thoughts on him romantically, picturing him as a possible suitor. Bloom watches her lift her leg suggestively—a gesture that appears to spur him to secretly masturbate.

This strange erotic moment, with Gerty making a flirtatious gesture and Bloom masturbating, is given additional climactic intensity as fireworks explode overhead in celebration of a Dublin bazaar.

The chapter then switches to Bloom's perspective, which is far more realistic than romantic, and as Gerty and her friends depart, he notices that she has a disabling limp. His denouement is offered in language very different from the earlier "Gerty" style, which Joyce, in a letter to his friend Frank Budgeon, described as "a namby-pamby jammy marmalady drawersy (alto lá!) style" (Ellmann 473). Bloom's thoughts are simple and weary, and so the chapter ends quietly, as Bloom drifts off into a "[s]hort snooze," as he calls it (312). This quiet ending will make the ensuing chapters all the more dramatic and sensational as the book's odyssey continues.

14. Oxen of the Sun

The next episode, chapter 14, takes place in the Holles Street maternity hospital. Bloom is there to inquire about Mrs. Purefoy, whose difficult childbirth is now in its third day. When he arrives, he runs into a young doctor named Dixon, who recently treated him for a bee sting at another hospital, and who invites him to join some young men drinking in a lounge, while he waits to hear news of Mrs. Purefoy. Stephen Dedalus is there, by now quite drunk, and we now have the two men, whose paths have crossed but never quite collided, meet up for the first time on this day.

The remainder of the chapter gives us the lively and sometimes raucous conversation in the room, much of it concerned with the topic of reproduction. It ends with the group's departure to a pub for additional drinks. Bloom, concerned about the inebriated Stephen, accompanies them, and when Stephen and his friend Lynch head off to the brothel district, Bloom continues to trail them. On a day when he has revisited the painful loss of his newborn son Rudy 11 years before, Bloom finds himself with an opportunity to play a paternal role to a young man in need of protection and support.

What transforms this arguably dull sounding series of events into a brilliantly exciting commentary is Joyce's transformation of the style of the chapter into a series of parodies of English literary styles beginning with Anglo-Saxon and evolving to the modern speech of the present moment of *Ulysses* at the beginning of the 20th century. In other words, Joyce stylistically mimics the development of the human infant in the womb from its embryonic beginnings to its birth with an evolving and changing prose, in which the events of the chapter are embedded. Terence Killeen explains what makes this chapter so difficult to read: "The 'story' has disappeared almost completely behind a screen far denser than any put up so far. It is, in fact, still going on, but it is almost invisible" (167).

We do get the "story," but in the language of different phases of English literary history. Bloom's arrival and meeting with Dixon recalls the treatment he received for a bee sting, but in language that now evokes medieval legends of knights battling dragons: "Leopold came there to be healed for he was sore wounded in his breast by a spear wherewith a horrible and dreadful dragon was smitten him" (317). A bit later, thunder is heard outside, and this evokes Norse mythology of "Thor thundered: in anger awful the hammerhurler," terrifying Stephen, and prompting "Master Bloom" to comfort him. Bloom reassures him that the "hubbub noise" is merely "the discharge of fluid from the thunderhead" and "all of the order of a natural phenomenon" (323).

A further focus on the weather is offered in the prosaic style of the 17th-century diaries of the English Member of Parliament, Samuel Pepys, beginning with the date: "So Thursday sixteenth June" and the main event: "Patk. Dignam laid in clay of an apoplexy," on a day when rain is badly needed after a drought, "The rosy buds all gone brown and spread out blobs and on the hills nought but dry flag and faggots that would catch at first fire" (324). When the style advances to the 18th century, so does the topic, turning to such racier issues as sexuality and reproduction. And here we get a bit of disconcerting information that Bloom apparently does not register. His daughter Milly's letter that morning alluded to a fellow named Bannon, and a planned picnic. And now a fellow named Bannon pipes up to tell of his encounter with a young woman who has just celebrated a birthday and wears a "new coquette cap" like the tam Bloom sent Milly as a birthday gift. Then, in the crafty 18th-century style that disguises sexual allusions with tropes, he reports that he is anguished because he forgot to bring a cloak: "Then, though it had poured seven showers, we were neither of us a penny the worse" (331). The cloak presumably refers to a forgotten condom, and if so, then Bloom's daughter may have lost her virginity and be in some peril of pregnancy. But Bloom appears not to track this conversation or connect it to his daughter, and at the end of the chapter, when, at the pub, Bannon suddenly recognizes that Bloom is Milly's father—"Bloo? Cadges ads. Photo's papli, by all that's gorgeous. Play low, pardner. Slide. *Bonsoir la compagnie"*(348)—he beats a hasty retreat.

We will never learn whether the Bloom family will end up with a crisis involving an unmarried 15-year-old daughter pregnant with a man who is off in the foreign service somewhere, and we can only hope this is not the outcome of the day.

15. Circe

The next chapter is the "Circe" episode, arguably the most dramatic one in *Ulysses*—not only thematically, but also stylistically, since it adopts the conventions of written drama, with characters presented as speakers, their actions as stage directions, and their words as dramatic dialogue.

The episode takes place in the red-light district of Dublin called "Nighttown" in *Ulysses*, at the brothel of a Mrs. Cohen on Tyrone Street. Bloom has at first lost sight of Stephen and Lynch, but soon finds and enters the brothel they are visiting. But even before this, he becomes engulfed in dramatic and unrealistic fantasies that will continue in wilder and raunchier form throughout the chapter.

In a sense, the Odyssean analogue for "Circe" predicts this. Odysseus and his men have landed on the island of a sorceress with the magical power to turn men into swine. This is the fate of Odysseus's men, who precede him to Circe's palace. Fortunately, on his way there Odysseus himself receives a magic herb called "moly" from Hermes. It allows him to repel Circe's magic and force her to turn his transformed crew back into men again, allowing them all to leave her island unscathed eventually.

Bloom is invited into Bella Cohen's brothel by an English prostitute named Zoe Higgins, and he finds Stephen and Lynch there engaged in verbal play with two women named Kitty and Florry. Bloom's first brothel fantasy acts out political dreams he might have had for himself of being an Irish hero. "My beloved subjects, a new era is about to dawn," he tells an adoring audience, "I, Bloom, tell you verily it is even now at hand. Yea, on the word of a Bloom, ye shall ere long enter into the golden city which is to be, the new Bloomusalem in the Nova Hibernia of the future" (395). However, this brilliant success soon takes a downward turn, as it historically did for Charles Stewart Parnell, with a mob yelling, "Lynch him! Roast him! He's as bad as Parnell was" (402).

In the real world of the brothel, Bloom seems to have been prating on about something, until Zoe puts an end to it by saying, "Talk away till you're black in the face" (407). Nonetheless, more fantasies ensue and they begin to take an erotic turn with the appearance of Bloom's grandfather, Lipoti Virag, who notes immediately that "Promiscuous nakedness is much in evidence hereabouts, eh?" (417). This sets the stage for the eventual appearance of the Madam—"*Bella Cohen, a massive whoremistress, enters*" (429) the stage directions tell us—who gestures to Bloom with her fan that she needs to have her bootlace tied. Once Bloom is on his knees to perform this task, it is not long before his masochistic fantasies turn the Madam into a masculinized dominatrix named "Bello," and Bloom himself into her cringing victim, bullied and degraded, who eventually confesses "O I have been a perfect pig" (449), turned into Circe's swine. The fantasy runs its course and Bloom emerges from it with his usual sobriety and good sense when Bella Cohen demands payment from the clients and appears to overcharge Stephen, something Bloom corrects. "You had better hand over that cash to me to take care of" (456), Bloom tells Stephen as he returns his money, now back in his paternal role.

Bloom's fantasies resume, however, and although they continue to cast him into a masochistic role as a liveried servant in his own home, the topic now becomes decidedly painful as he is obliged to usher his rival Boylan in to see his own wife. "Hello, Bloom! Mrs Bloom dressed yet?" Boylan shouts as he jumps from his car and the servile Bloom replies, "Yes, sir. Madam Tweedy is in her bath, sir" (461). Boylan generously offers to let him watch, "You can apply your eye to the keyhole and play with yourself while I just go through her a few times" (462), and Bloom appears to do so with "*eyes wildly dilated.*"

Although Bloom has fretted about Boylan's afternoon visit to Molly all day, this fantasy represents his first visualization of the affair, a confrontation—even if unconscious—that may actually have a perverse therapeutic effect and make him realize he needs to do something to get his relationship with Molly back on track. Bloom is not the only one to experience fantasies here, however, for soon Stephen's begin as well. The party turns playful and festive when Zoe drops some coins into the pianola, and encourages everyone to dance to the tune of "My girl's a Yorkshire girl" (471).

But for Stephen the dance soon becomes a "Dance of death," and death conjures up his mother, whose appearance causes Stephen, "*choking in fright, remorse, and horror,*" to cry out: "They say I killed you, mother. He offended your memory. Cancer did it, not I. Destiny" (474). The Mother urges him to "Repent, Stephen," and begins to frighten him when she approaches him with "*smouldering eyes,*" until he can no longer bear it. He turns on her, shouting, "*Non serviam,*" then smashes the salon's chandelier with his walking stick.

The party has come to an end, Stephen runs out, and Bella Cohen furiously demands an excessive payment for the broken lamp. Bloom pays only what he thinks is owed, and runs out to catch up with Stephen, who has entered into an altercation with two British soldiers. Bloom tries to intervene and get Stephen to leave: "Come along with me now before worse happens. Here's your stick" (490), but Private Carr punches Stephen in the face and knocks him out. The police arrive and Bloom worries that Stephen may be arrested, but a fellow he knows who has just arrived intervenes and gets the officers to back off. Stephen gradually becomes conscious again and then goes back to sleep. As Bloom wistfully looks at him, he suddenly has a vision of his own son as he might be now, "*a fairy boy of eleven*," holding a book in his hand and reading it, as if it were in Hebrew "*"from right to left inaudibly, smiling, kissing the page,"* causing Bloom to say his name, "Rudy!" (497).

Book III

16. Eumaeus

Book II comes to an end with this dramatic ending of "Circe," and Book III commences, with the surprisingly uneventful and stylistically simple episode called "Eumaeus."

Bloom has helped the now conscious but unsteady Stephen to his feet, and hearing him ask for something to drink takes him to a cabman's shelter for a cup of coffee. On the way there they run into a fellow named Corley, familiar to readers of *Dubliners*, and known to Stephen, if not to Bloom. Corley is apparently just as penniless as he was then, and tries to borrow money from Stephen and get advice on possible jobs.

The chapter, with its early reference to Bloom as a good "Samaritan" (501) and allusions to the poverty-stricken members of society aided by the Salvation Army's charity, is focused on a neglected and forgotten part of the social world. The Odyssean reference for this episode relates Odysseus's return to Ithaca, where he is obliged to disguise himself and take refuge with Eumaeus, a swineherd who once worked for him, and who treats him kindly. After Odysseus reveals himself to Eumaeus, they are joined by Telemachus, who does not recognize his father until he reveals himself, and together they plan a strategy for reclaiming the palace.

The analogies between the Joycean and Homeric versions are a bit sketchier than they are in other chapters, but the basic element is there: Bloom, discovering that Stephen will not return to the Martello tower or to his father's home, offers to take him back to his own home on Eccles Street. The "reunion" of the modern day "father" and "son" is not particularly uplifting in this episode. Bloom tries to ply Stephen with good advice, suggesting one can live well if "you work," to which Stephen replies "Count me out" (526). Bloom points out that he means work in the widest sense, including literary work, or writing for a newspaper, for example. "You have every bit as much right to live by your pen in pursuit of your philosophy as the peasant has," Bloom tells him, since both writer and peasant, brain and brawn, belong to Ireland. Stephen rudely dismisses this notion, saying "We can't change the country. Let us change the subject" (527).

Fatherhood is not an easy task, this portion of the episode makes clear. Nonetheless, his engagement with Stephen in the cabman's shelter lets Bloom confide his views, arguably more successfully than at others times in his day. He tells Stephen of the citizen's anti-Semitic attack on him, reporting with some pride his retort, "So I without deviating from plain facts in the least told him his God, I mean Christ, was a jew too." "Am I not right?" (525). Although Stephen's response concurs, it is made in a style Bloom may not grasp immediately, since it is offered in words from the Latin Vulgate: "*Ex quibus*, Stephen mumbled in a noncommittal accent," followed by the words *Christus secundum carnem*. Don Gifford and Robert Seidman translate this as "and from that race [the Israelites] is Christ" in their note in *'Ulysses' Annotated* (549). Stephen could just have said "Yes" rather than showing off his erudition. Conversation between Bloom and Stephen is not easy in this chapter.

Joyce appears to pursue a number of agendas in this episode. The most prominent, as I have noted, is that surrogate fatherhood does not start out as a sentimentally satisfying experience for Bloom. And Stephen, who might appear an excellent candidate as an intelligent surrogate son, is not in the best spirits or on his most courteous or engaging behavior after his tumultuous and stressful day.

But the episode also allows for the introduction of a slew of complicated lower-class characters, including the jobless Corley, the intriguing sailor D.B. Murphy—who may or may not be who he says he is—and the mysterious keeper of the establishment, who may or may not be Skin-the-Goat, the driver of a decoy car in the Phoenix Park murders incident of 1882. Even Bloom's identity becomes muddled when he is listed in the evening newspaper's obituary of Paddy

Dignam's funeral as the attendee named "*L. Boom*" (529). The most woeful of the poor figures on the scene, who is not even permitted to enter the cabman's shelter, is a haggard streetwalker in a black straw hat, presumably a former prostitute evicted from her brothel on account of syphilis, who is now homeless and who tries to survive by begging people to let her do their washing.

This world represents the social underside of society that persons like Bloom and Stephen encounter only on the margins of their experience, on a night like this. In addition to this social expansion, Joyce also continues his stylistic experiment in this chapter in a form that Terence Killeen considers "the most extraordinary" in *Ulysses*, even though it is prosaic and conspicuously ordinary. The events are recounted by a narrator who draws attention to the fact that he is telling his story by correcting some false information he may have given his reader or listener about some distant ancestral relative of Corley's (504) and thereby also makes us self-conscious about our role as listeners to his account. His language is peppered with qualifications of what he tells us, as when he adds "not to put too fine a point on it" (502) to a statement, or "[t]hough this sort of thing went on every other night or very near it" (505) to add perspective to an event. He does not mind characterizing the people he talks about, saying of "Murphy:" "Whilst speaking he produced a dangerouslooking claspknife quite in keeping with his character and held it in the striking position" (514), and even giving the supposed sailor a nickname, "Shipahoy of course had his own say to say" (521). And he makes it difficult for us to decide whether he is clever or not at all clever, as when he characterizes Bloom as throwing "a nasty sidelight on that side of a person's character, no pun intended."

Terence Killeen reverses often held views that this narrative voice is as tired as Stephen and Bloom after their long day, by arguing that the style is "in fact, extremely active, indeed tireless" (205).

17. Ithaca

The stylistic change that marks the next chapter, "Ithaca," is as dramatic as the one we previously encountered in "Aeolus," because the text is immediately distinguished by being written in a question and answer format. "What parallel courses did Bloom and Stephen follow returning?" (544), the first voice asks and answers, and then goes on to pose a long string of questions and answers until the end of the episode.

The traditional model for such a textual question and answer design is, of course, the Catholic catechism, which traditionally relies on this format for presenting the church's doctrines to children and adult converts so that they can memorize the correct responses. In this form, the Catechism presents itself as indisputably true and immune to questioning. In this respect, Joyce turns the "Ithaca" catechism upside down, by making its responses problematic in multiple ways—sometimes vague, sometimes irrelevant, sometimes inaccurate and marked by critical omissions, and therefore designed to evoke just those doubts and disputes that the Catechism is designed to block.

Relating this stylistic complexity to the Homeric parallel is therefore also challenging. Understanding that Stephen has no place to go, Bloom takes him from the cabman's shelter to his home at 7 Eccles Street, where he lets himself in by lowering himself and jumping from the inside of the fence by the front steps into the lower area that leads into the kitchen. This is necessary because Bloom left his house key in his other pants when he donned a black outfit for the impending funeral visit that morning.

Bloom and Stephen appear to have had friendlier discussions on the way to Bloom's house. After preparing and offering Stephen some hot cocoa, the two men continue to develop an amiable conversation that becomes quite jolly until it hits a surprising and disconcerting snag during an initially playful moment when they exchange songs related to each man's race or ethnicity. Bloom sings the Zionist national anthem. Stephen responds by singing a horrible anti-Semitic ballad about a little boy named Harry Hughes who accidentally breaks the window of the home of a Jew, whose daughter invites Harry into the house and cuts off his head.

Joyce clearly wanted readers to pay attention to the ballad because it is printed both in italics and as a musical score with the lyrics written in Joyce's own handwriting (566-7). We desperately need the Catechism at this point to explain to us why Stephen would sing such a song to a Jewish man. However, the answers fail miserably, telling us only that the ballad made Bloom, "the father of Millicent," very sad, but giving us a troublingly unclear summary of Stephen's commentary on the ballad. He appears to treat the victim in the ballad as possibly having courted his fate, "It leads him to a strange habitation, to a secret infidel apartment, and there, implacable, immolates him, consenting" (567). Is Stephen referring to himself here, as a consenting victim of the man who saved him from having his money depleted by a greedy brothel madam and kept him from being arrested?

Critics inevitably struggle to come up with a reasonable interpretation, creating a variety of complex possibilities. Scholar Neil

Davison, for instance, sees Stephen's ballad as representing to him "his own victimization as a son, an outcast, and an Irishman," thereby suggesting that Bloom in his Jewishness is in a similar situation. "Stephen feels he has escaped his own victimization, and seems to imply that Bloom should follow suit" (234). On the other hand, author Paul Schwaber suggests that "neither Stephen nor Leopold aimed to feel much during that strange moment, that their respective defenses against tumult—Stephen repressing and intellectualizing, Bloom obsessing and digressing—served each of them well just then" (189). I would argue that there is no simple explanation of the motive or justification of Stephen's act and that of the ballad itself, and that leaving it mysterious may have been the point. Perhaps its function at a time when anti-Semitism was a not uncommon feature of modernist writing, was to urge readers to explore and deplore its possible causes and explanations and consider its possibly disastrous effects.

The chapter continues with a further surprise, as Bloom, the troublesome ballad notwithstanding, offers Stephen the chance to spend the night in a spare room in his home. Given what has just transpired, this is very kind, and yet Bloom's offer of asylum is "[p]romptly, inexplicably, with amicability, gratefully" declined by Stephen (570). This too is surprising since, given his situation, he has no place to go on this night. We know he had a row of some sort with Mulligan at the train station, and when Bloom asked Stephen at the cabman's shelter where his father lived, his response was "in Dublin somewhere" (507), implying that he may not even know his address.

Where Stephen spends the remainder of this night will remain one of the many unsolved mysteries in *Ulysses*. Bloom and Stephen part ways amicably after quietly urinating in the garden, and Bloom now goes back inside to get undressed and get into bed, where he kisses Molly's bottom and thereby wakes her up, causing her to interrogate what he has been doing this evening until such a late hour. And so, lying on opposite sides of the bed, with Bloom's head by Molly's feet and vice versa, Bloom goes to sleep while Molly, wide awake, launches into the thoughts that comprise the last chapter of *Ulysses*.

So what does all of this have to do with the *Odyssey*? Homer ends his epic saga by having Odysseus, Telemachus, and Eumaeus return to his palace in Ithaca, where Penelope tests her possible suitors by requiring them to shoot an arrow through the holes of a series of arranged axe-handles, a feat she knows only her husband can successfully accomplish. The suitors inevitably fail while Odysseus succeeds, and the suitors are now at his mercy, Telemachus having locked the door to block their escape. The suitors are murdered, Odysseus fumigates the palace (Bloom lights an incense cone before going to the bedroom, 580), and prepares to join Penelope who, not sure of his identity as her husband, proposes to have the marriage bed moved outside the sleeping chamber on this night. Odysseus angrily tells her that this is impossible because he built the bed himself and it is constructed out of a living olive tree and cannot be moved. His revelation of this secret convinces Penelope that Odysseus is indeed her husband, and the couple is now reunited.

In *Ulysses* the slaying of the suitors takes place in Bloom's head, in his possible willingness to understand his wife's infidelity in the context of their marital difficulties, and his seemingly tacit decision not to accuse or reprove her for the events in their home on this day. The secret of the marriage bed appears to be the buried knowledge in each member of the couple that their sexual problems are rooted not in any dislike they have for each other, or in a lack of sexual attraction, but in the tragedy of losing a son. This shared understanding promises to pave the way to a possible forgiveness and reconciliation.

18. Penelope

And so we come to "Penelope," the last and most famous chapter of *Ulysses*, presented as a first-person rumination of Molly's day and her life. Her thoughts are presented in eight long paragraphs, if we can call them that, distinguished by their lack of punctuation, quotation marks, or capital letters as a new sentence or new paragraph begins. The first-person voice is not really a narration because it is not directed at any listener except the self, and is therefore entirely interiorized and private. This allows it to be entirely free and unrestrained, which accounts for the frankness, boldness, and unembarrassed bawdiness that Molly's thoughts express.

Molly has a strong personality and an interesting and complicated background. She grew up on the island of Gibraltar where her father served as a Major in the British army, and her mother was a "Spanish Jewess" named Lunita Loredo, whose community would have "considered mixed marriage an anathema," according to author Phillip Herring (*Joyce's Uncertainty Principle* 133). There is virtually no action in this chapter except for a brief moment when Molly gets out of bed and urinates in a chamber pot. It is, therefore, complicated to discern Homeric parallels, which must ultimately be found in the character and the style of Joyce's Penelope, rather than in the episode's events.

In the *Odyssey*, Penelope initially puts off the demands of her suitors by pleading for time to weave a shroud for her aging father-in-law, which she unravels every night, and begins weaving again in the morning. This strategy of weaving and unraveling is unconscious and mental on Molly's part, as she creates a line of thought, then takes it apart with digression and veering into other topics, only to return and resume the original concern. Penelope's challenge to the suitors has no clear parallel although Molly's suitors, past and present, surface in her thoughts. She actually remembers her first boyfriend Mulvey fondly, and remains saddened that the British Lieutenant Gardner, with whom she appears to have had a romantic connection, died in the Boer war. Bloom's and his wife's reaction to another fellow who had a one-time interest in Molly sharply illustrates the differences in their personalities. Bloom is almost forgiving of Menton's rudeness to him after the funeral that morning ("Never mind. Be sorry after perhaps when it dawns on him" 95), while Molly blasts Menton for coming on to her those many years ago ("he had the impudence to make up to me one time well done to him mouth almighty and his boiled eyes of all the big stupoes I ever met" 609). But it is, of course, Boylan who is the suitor at issue on this day, since he is Molly's first adulterous lover who clearly surprised and pleased her with his sexual prowess.

The Homeric parallel does surface here, for although Molly has many complimentary things to say about Boylan, she ultimately dismisses him as a potential partner and mocks him as an "ignoramus" who has "no manners nor no refinement nor no nothing," a man who "doesnt know poetry from a cabbage" (638), unlike her much more polite and genteel husband. Comparing Bloom to other spouses she notes, "Poldy anyhow whatever he does always wipes his feet on the mat when he comes in wet or shine and always blacks his own boots too" (613). And she vigorously defends him against the disparagement of "goodfornothings," noting "he has sense enough not to squander every penny piece he earns down their gullets and looks after his wife and family" (636).

Homer's Penelope appears to devise the frustration of her suitors to create the time and opportunity for her husband to return to her from the Trojan War. In *Ulysses*, this is echoed in Molly's strong focus on Bloom throughout her thoughts, making it clear that she wants nothing more than to have him return to her in the fullest marital way with the sexual satisfaction they enjoyed before the tragedy of Rudy interfered with it. It is almost as though she has begun the affair with Boylan as a wake-up call to her husband, to get him to see that he may lose her if he doesn't deal with their situation. Given that their entire sexual crisis was triggered by the loss of a son, Bloom's acquisition of a surrogate, even if only for a day, could conceivably make a change or resolution possible, and if so, the ending of Molly's musings make it clear that nothing would make her happier. She looks forward to shopping and preparing a lovely dinner the following evening in the event Stephen returns to join them, and she goes back in her mind to Bloom's sweet courtship of her, "the sun shines for you he said the day we were lying among the rhododendrons on Howth head" (643).

The novel ends with Molly going to sleep remembering the day Bloom proposed to her, and in that tender and loving moment asked her "to say yes my mountain flower and first I put my arms around him yes and drew him down to me so he could feel my breasts all perfume yes and his heart was going like mad and yes I said yes I will Yes" (644).

5

Finnegans Wake

Finnegans Wake was Joyce's last work, published in 1939, two years before his death in 1941. Like the groundbreaking *Ulysses*, the *Wake*, as we now refer to it, was completely avant-garde at the time of its publication, a work so unconventional that it is impossible to classify it by genre as a novel. It is poetic, yet with too much narrative to be considered purely as poetry, and it is written in English of sorts, although its words are often overlaid with echoes and spellings of other languages.

Joyce scholar and critic Kimberly Devlin points out that "The logic of the *Wake* has long been recognized as being rooted in elaborate puns, verbal coincidences and contiguities" (*Wandering and Return in 'Finnegans Wake'* 13). But as its title suggests, the work does have a theme of sorts that may be traced back to one of its inspirations, an Irish ballad titled "Finnegan's Wake," with the apostrophe missing from Joyce's book, which multiplies the name of Finnegan as it multiplies pretty much everything in the work.

The ballad tells the story of a drunken hod carrier, who falls and dies after carrying bricks up a ladder. He is, however, resurrected at his wake, giving "wake" the double meaning of a raucous celebration of the dead and its reversal or revival as he "wakes" from the dead. One way to account for both the complicated form of the work and its layered themes and characters is to think of it as a *dream*, a work inspired by the way our dreams take the materials of everyday life and transform them into something new and mysterious that nonetheless retains an oblique relationship to the ordinary. John Bishop's *Joyce's Book of the Dark: 'Finnegans Wake'* recounts how Joyce explained to friends that his new work would follow *Ulysses*, his book of the day, with a new book of the night (4).

Joyce was inspired by a variety of thinkers and works in creating it, including the Italian philosopher Giambattista Vico, the psychoanalyst Sigmund Freud, and an ancient work titled *The Egyptian Book of the Dead*. Thematically the work can be said to revolve around a family with a nurturing mother, a father who is in trouble—perhaps for a crime of some sort—twin sons who are at odds with each other, and a daughter. These figures are given not only many names but also non-human incarnations: the mother as a river or a hen, for example, the father as land, the sons as an ant and a grasshopper, and the daughter as a cloud. Because these layered identities make it difficult to talk about them, critics have whittled their names down to a simpler format, with the father most generally referred to as Humphrey Chimpden Earwicker or HCE, the mother as Anna Livia Plurabelle or ALP, the sons as Shem and Shaun, and the daughter as Isabel.

An early introductory study by Joseph Campbell and Henry Morton Robinson called *A Skeleton Key to 'Finnegans Wake'* discusses the work systematically by following its structure of four books of very different lengths. The first book contains eight chapters, the second and third consist of four chapters each, and the fourth book contains only a single chapter. My discussion will inevitably focus on the first book at greater length than the others, but will encompass some discussion of each of the *Wake's* four books.

Book I

The *Wake* begins in mid-sentence with the un-capitalized word "riverrun," as an unidentifiable voice describes a geographic landscape that we can recognize as Dublin, its river Liffey winding toward the landmark of "Howth Castle and Environs," whose capital letters point to the initials of a figure later identified as HCE (*Finnegans Wake* 3). This male figure, often described as lying on his back, is identified with the landscape, while his always-in-motion wife Anna Livia Plurabelle is identified with the river Liffey.

The next paragraph evokes narratives from various mythologies, with "Sir Tristram" perhaps alluding to the Celtic story of the lovers Tristan and Isolde, "tauftauf thuartpeatrick" making reference to the baptism of the Irish Saint Patrick, and "a kidscad buttended a bland old isaac" evoking the biblical story of Esau and Jacob and their father Isaac. The mention of an "arclight," and a "regginbrow" suggests an allusion to the story of Noah's ark, which survives the biblical deluge that is followed by a rainbow. The third paragraph now introduces "The fall (bababadalgharaghtakamminarronnkonnbronntonnerronntuonnthunntrovarrhounawnskawntoohoohoordenenthurnuk!)" (3), whose strange one-hundred letter parenthetical description represents a thunderclap. Campbell and Robinson construe this as the racket made by Finnegan falling from the ladder, but it may also refer to Giambattista Vico's theory about the first age of man, the age of giants, when God used a ferocious thunderbolt to frighten the savages into forging a more orderly and civilized life. We remember now an early allusion to "Eve and Adam's" in the first sentence of the *Wake*, a reference to Adam and Eve's church in Dublin, but also to the fall of the biblical Adam and Eve. The "fall" is therefore an important theme in the work with both physical and moral connotations.

This brief and cursory description of just the first page, and just the first three paragraphs of the 628-page long *Finnegans Wake*, hopefully gives a hint of the enormous complexity of the work, at the same time that it makes clear that the text is not nonsense but has topics and themes and motifs that relate coherently to one another. It simply takes time, experience, and the help of aids like the *Skeleton Key* for the reader to sort things out.

On the next page of the first chapter (4) we receive a clearer description of the fall of the hod carrier "Bygmester Finnegan," who appears to be climbing a structure as tall as a Woolworth skyscraper—"a waalworth of a skyerscape"—from which either objects like tools, or men like Laurence O'Toole, go "clittering up" and "clottering down" (5). This is followed by a question about what caused the fellow's tragedy and "sin business," suggesting there may be "one thousand and one stories" (the number of the *Arabian Nights*) needed to explain it. A wake ("Fillagain's chrissormiss wake" [6]) follows, in which the fallen man is mourned, "Macool, Macool, orra whyi deed ye diie?," at the same time that a board is spread with food and drinks for the mourners, "Grampupus is fallen down but grinny sprids the boord" (7).

The scene soon changes to a tour of the Wellington Museum (or "museyroom") in Dublin's Phoenix Park, with a guide pointing out exhibits from the Napoleonic wars (8-10). Once back outside, we now encounter one of ALP's incarnations in the form of a little hen, a "gnarlybird ygathering," searching for food in rhythms of pecking, "runalittle, doalittle, preealittle, pouralittle, wipealittle, kicksalittle" (10)—although in her human incarnation, her gathering includes cartridges and buttons, diapers, maps, pennies, brooches, garters, shoes, weapons, and many other objects: "all spoiled goods go into her nabsack" (11). While her husband sleeps, ALP makes a fire and prepares breakfast, including "iggs" served "sunny side up with care" (12).

Further on in the chapter we meet the sons in the form of

primitive cavemen named "Mutt" and "Jute," who initially have trouble speaking, with "mutter" and "stummer" coming from the "utterer" (16). Still further, we are given a story about the encounter of a Jarl van Hoother with a female figure called the "prankquean" (21-23), who kidnaps his sons one at a time when she is refused a glass of porter. Echoes of the ballad return with mourners encouraging Finnegan to stay dead and not wake up, "Now be aisy, good Mr Finnimore, sir. And take your laysure like a god on pension and don't be walking abroad" (24). A little later they recur again, "Aisy now, you decent man, with your knees and lie quiet and repose your honour's lordship" (27).

The chapter culminates with the announcement that a new fellow has arrived, one with a wife and two sons and a daughter. The familiar initials identify him as the figure we will come to know as HCE, an "old offender" who was "humile, commune and ensectuous from his nature" and who will be "ultimendly respunchable for the hubbub caused in Edenborough" (29). Campbell and Robinson note that "HCE has supplanted Finnegan" (55).

And so chapter 1 ends and the second chapter begins with a promise to tell us about "the genesis of Harold or Humphrey Chimpden's occupational agnomen" (30). Working in an Eden-like garden "in prefall paradise peace," royalty is announced to him by a runner. The Humphrey or Harold figure dresses up and bearing a pole topped with a flower pot goes to greet his "majesty," who asks him a question about the preferable bait for "lobstertrapping." He answers that he was just catching some earwigs, "Naw, yer maggers, aw war jist a cotchin on thon bluggy earwuggers" (31), and with this response "Haromphrey" is given "the sigla H.C.E.". This results in "the nickname Here Comes Everybody" (32), and he becomes loved as "the big cleanminded giant H. C. Earwicker" (33).

But soon questions are raised about this fellow, slander is insinuated, and other stories about him are told. One of them entails his encounter on a walk in a park with "a cad with a pipe" (35). The man asks HCE to tell him the time, to which HCE responds by looking at his watch, telling the fellow the time, and then defending himself against all the slander to which he has been subjected. This leads the cad to go home and recount the strange meeting to himself over drinks at supper, only to be overheard by his wife who, in turn, tells her priest, trusting him to keep it confidential. The priest, however, tells it to a man while laying bets at a racetrack, and is overheard by two other fellows. As a result the whole story is eventually transformed into a ballad called "The Ballad of Persse O'Reilly" (44). This begins with the story of Humpty Dumpty's fall from "the Magazine Wall" in Phoenix Park, and ends with the prediction that unlike Finnegan, HCE will not rise again, "And not all the king's men nor his horses/ Will resurrect his corpus" (47).

Up to this point there has been a certain clarity about the story of HCE, but in the third and fourth chapters that clarity will disappear and be replaced by multiple versions and accounts, by doubts and questions raised about all of the characters, creating an irresolvable confusion, a "spoof of visibility in a freakfog" as the first sentence of chapter 3 calls it (48). We are supposedly given a follow up on the fates of "the persins sin this Eyrawyggla saga." Though it is described as "readable," it is also from top to bottom "all falsetissues," and so we are told nothing of any certainty. Given "the wet and low visibility" (51) of the setting, it is even impossible to "idendifine the individuone" who was asked to tell "that fishabed ghoatstory of the haardly creditable edventyres of the Haberdasher, the two Curchies and the three Enkelchums".

HCE's adventures are here described as hardly credible, their story-teller impossible to identify, their account no more than fish stories or ghost stories, and the protagonist himself split into five different entities. No wonder we are not going to get any solutions to anything in this chapter. "Thus the unfacts, did we posses them, are too imprecisely few to warrant our certitude, the evidencegivers by legpoll too untrustworthily irreperible" (57). But although we learn nothing usable about the facts of the story, we are given some intriguing allusions, including one to the "sixes and seventies" of "Halley's comet" (54), which has a 76-year period and made an appearance in April 1910. There is also a reference to "Television" (52), a medium apparently talked about as early as the 1920s, even if not available until after Joyce's time.

Chapter 4 offers to "Let us leave theories there and return to here's here" (76), a present time in which the father figure appears to be dead and in his "teak coffin," with all sorts of funerary equipment about: "Show coffins, winding sheets, goodbuy bierchepes, cinerary urns" (77) and more. But, of course, in *Finnegans Wake* the dead may always "rise afterfall" (78). As a result, previous events will be revisited, more conflicts and trials will be conducted, and the wife—now named "Kate Strong, a widow" (79), will still be found scavenging around "her filthdump near the Serpentine in Phornix Park" (80). At some point we are told "And so it all ended" (93), even though it clearly hasn't, and we now get mention of "The letter! The litter!" perhaps found in the midden heap or dump. By the end of the chapter, the focus will have shifted to the wife and mother: "But there's a little lady waiting and her name is A.L.P." (102), and she will defend her husband. "Then who but Crippled-with-Children would speak up for Dropping-with-Sweat?" (102). And so we come to chapter 5, generally regarded as "the letter chapter."

It begins with a religious invocation, "In the name of Annah the Allmaziful, the Everliving, the Bringer of Plurabilities, haloed be her eve, her singtime sung, her rill be run, unhemmed as it is uneven" (104). And "plurabilities" or plural possibilities are what we will get once more, beginning with a barrage of titles for the letter. "Her untitled mamafesta memorialising the Mosthighest has gone by many names at disjointed times," we are told, and the italicized list which goes on for three pages includes a self-reflexive title, "*This Funnycoon's Week*" (105), an allusion to Tristan and Isolde, "*Armoury Treestam and Icy Siseule*" (104), a reference to Humpty Dumpty's fall, "*Lumptytumtumpty had a Big Fall*" (106), and reference to a play presented by the children in the first chapter of Book II.

We may expect to have the themes we have encountered so far revisited, "a multiplicity of personalities inflicted on the documents or document" and their "prevision of virtual crime or crimes" (107). But instead, the chapter proceeds to analyze the letter largely for its material detail. The writing is described as a "proteiform graph" that itself is a "polyhedron of scripture" (107). The letter appears to avoid citation, and "inferring from the nonpresence of inverted commas (sometimes called quotation marks)" the narrative voice suggests that "its author was always constitutionally incapable of misappropriating the spoken words of others" (108). The discussion directs its focus on the nature of "a quite everydaylooking stamped addressed envelope" and argues that even though it is only an "outer husk," it nonetheless deserves attention because "to concentrate solely on the literal sense or even the psychological content" of the "enveloping facts themselves" is "hurtful to sound sense" (109).

But then the narrator turns back to "that original hen," describing her as "a cold fowl" in "Midwinter" (110) and now gives her a name: "The bird in the case was Belinda of the Dorans" (111). She scratches at "the hour of klokking twelve" and finds a "goodish-sized sheet of letterpaper originating by transcript from Boston (Mass.)". We now get a sense of the content of the letter addressed to "Dear whom it proceded to mention"—although we are not given the name of the recipient. It then talks about "Maggy well & allathome's health well," alludes to "*the van* Houtens," mentions "a beautiful present of wedding cakes for dear thankyou Chriesty," remembers the "grand funferall of poor Father Michael," asks "well how are you Maggy & hopes soon to hear well & must now close it with fondest to the twoinns with four crosskisses" (111). The letter is apparently marked by a large "teastain" which certifies it as a "genuine relique of ancient Irish pleasant pottery" (111). Later, this teastain is revisited again in a discussion about what appears to be the absence of a signature, perhaps because "it was a habit not to sign letters always" (114), and the question is raised "So why, pray, sign anything as long as every word, letter, penstroke, paperspace, is a perfect signature of its own?" (115). The letter chapter goes on a bit longer and then ends with reference to one of the Earwicker sons, "that odious and still today insufficiently malestimated note-snatcher" known as "Shem the Penman" (125).

We might reasonably expect the next chapter to deal with Shem the Penman, but that discussion is postponed until chapter 7. Chapter 6 is known as "the quiz" chapter, a series of 12 questions and answers that deal with the characters, themes, places, and events that have been recurring in previous episodes. Critic Patrick McCarthy reminds us that this question and answer format is not new in Joyce's work, and that the "Ithaca" chapter of *Ulysses* had a similar catechism design (47). But the questions and answers here vary wildly.

In a gloss on Finnegan's climb up and fall down, the first question relates to a fellow who rose higher than a beanstalk or the Wellington monument, and then goes on for more than 13 pages only to give us his identity in a brief answer: "Finn MacCool" (139). The second query, on the other hand, is simple, "Does your mutter know your mike?"—a question ostensibly posed to Shaun, according to Campbell and Robinson, and answered with echoes of a song called "The Shandon Bells" (108). It is difficult to make sense of the questions or the answers, as these examples show. The fourth question (140) asks about an "Irish capitol city" of "two syllables and six letters," and while Dublin of course comes immediately to mind, we are given a choice of four answers: a) Delfas (Belfast, according to Campbell and Robinson), b) Dorhqk (Cork), c) Nublid (Dublin) and d) Dalway (Galway). Question 8 asks "And how war yore maggies?" and offers the charming reply that "They war loving, they love laughing, they laugh weeping, they weep smelling, they smell smiling, they smile hating, they hate thinking, they think feeling, they feel tempting, they tempt daring, they dare waiting," and so on and so forth (142). Question 9 asks what a person fatigued at night might see, perhaps in sleep, and the answer suggests motions and colors characteristic of a "collideorscape"

(143) or the kaleidoscope of the *Wake* itself. The next question begins with a romantic lament: "What bitter's love but yurning," which is given a highly personal response. "I know, pipette, of course, dear, but listen, precious," the male voice says, and goes on to pay compliments and give advice.

The 11th question is posed in the poetic rhythms of the late 18th century Scottish poet Thomas Campbell's "*The Exile of Erin,*" according to Campbell and Robinson (110), and asks if one fellow would help another in need, only to be given the answer "No, blank ye!" (149). But the reply, if it is given by Shaun, goes on for about nineteen pages, and encompasses a lecture by a "Professor Loewy-Brueller" (150) that includes the fable of the "The Mookse and The Gripes" (152), a play on Aesop's "The Fox and the Grapes," with allusions to Irish political history. A female figure in the shape of a cloud named Nuvoletta is introduced into the Mookse and Gripes fable (157), and although she does her best to charm them ("she tried to make the Mookse look up at her" and tried "to make the Gripes hear how coy she could be") she fails (157). The Mookse is "not amoosed" and the Gripes remains "pinefully obliviscent" (158). The brother theme is replayed again with two figures named "Burrus" and "Caseous," and a girl named "Marge" or "Margareen," suggesting that we are dealing here with a bit of a love triangle between butter, cheese, and margarine. "Margareena she's very fond of Burrus but, alick and alack! she velly fond of chee" (166).

The chapter ends with further allusions to the conflict between the brothers ("were we bread by the same fire and signed with the same salt"), who nonetheless declare a curious unity in the end although one that foregrounds Shem: "*Semus sumus!*" (168) or "We are Shem!" according to Campbell and Robinson (123).

We now come to the penultimate chapter of Book I, the "Shem chapter." The episode will indeed focus on Shem, but it appears to be narrated by his enemy twin Shaun. As a result, Shaun is as much present in the critical and deprecating narrative voice of the chapter as is his subject, Shem, whose reputation is attacked right from the start.

Shem may have come from "respectable stemming," but now "his back life will not stand being written about in black and white." His physical description is entirely negative, telling us he has "one numb arm up a sleeve," "not a foot to stand on, a handful of thumbs, a blind stomach, a deaf heart, a loose liver, two fifths of two buttocks" and "a bladder tristened," among other unattractive features (169). His character is equally maligned: "Shem was a sham and a low sham and his lowness creeped out first via foodstuffs" since he prefers tinned salmon to "the plumpest roeheavy lax" and canned pineapple to its "junglegrown" variety (170). Indeed, "he would far sooner muddle through the hash of lentils in Europe than meddle with Irrland's split little pea" (171)—an allusion hinting at James Joyce himself, who preferred to spend most of his adult life in Europe rather than in Ireland.

Campbell and Robinson note that Shem, as the penman, "is, in fact, as the reader will immediately perceive, James Joyce himself" (123). But the narrative voice gives him little credit for his poetic skills, and predicts that it will "trickle out" that he was "in his bardic memory low" (172). Like his persecuted father, Shem is also beset by enemies obliging him to cork himself up in "his inkbattle house," his inkbottle, but also his writing career, in fear for his life, "afar for the life" (176). On a day described as "that bloody, Swithun's day, though every doorpost in muchtried Lucalizod was smeared with generous erstborn gore," Shem in a "thorough fright" stays hidden in his room, checking on the events outside only by looking through his "westernmost keyhole" with an "eighteen hawkspower durdicky telescope"—a disastrous move since he finds himself "at pointblank range blinking down the barrel of an irregular revolver" (178-179). The weapon is handled by "an unkown quarreler" who has apparently been "told off to shade and shoot shy Shem should the shit show his shiny shnout" (179). Shem's house, known as "the Haunted Inkbottle" (182), is later described as having its floor and walls "literatured with burst loveletters, telltale stories, stickyback snaps, doubtful eggshells" and much more, including "once current puns, quashed quotatoes, messes of mottage, unquestionable issue papers, seedy ejaculations, limerick damns, crocodile tears, spilt ink," and on and on (183).

The chapter ends with speeches from two figures, first JUSTIUS, who seems to speak in the voice of Shaun, and then MERCIUS, the voice of Shem, which is much more self-deprecating than that of his judgmental brother. The latter calls himself a "branded sheep, pick of the wasterpaperbaskel," announcing the arrival of their mother, "little oldfashioned mummy, little wonderful mummy, ducking under bridges, bellhopping the weirs, dodging by a bit of bog" (194). This will be Anna Livia Plurabelle, the woman who is also a river, and who will be the subject of the final chapter of Book I.

The most famous chapter in the book begins with a narrative voice saying "O/ tell me all about/ Anna Livia!/ I want to hear all/ about Anna Livia" (196). We soon determine that this voice is in dialogue with another speaker, who does indeed begin to talk about Anna Livia, while reminding her interlocutor to "Wash quit and don't be dabbling. Tuck up your sleeves and loosen your talktapes" (196).

Joyce biographer Richard Ellmann reports that Joyce described the chapter to his patron Harriet Shaw Weaver as "a chattering dialogue across the river by two washerwomen who as night falls become a tree and a stone" (563). The two washerwomen are doing laundry in the waters of the flowing river, who is Anna Livia Plurabelle or the river Liffey herself. Not only is the figure of their discussion fluid, but so is the story, its telling, and its language. Ellmann notes that on the night Joyce finished the chapter, he went down to the river Seine to listen to the sound of the water to make sure he got the description of the sound right. "He came back content," Ellmann writes (564 n.50).

In a sense, the river dominates the chapter in its form as the fluid female protagonist, the topic of conversation. Its language offers the sound of flowing water reflected in the flow of the prose, and in the names of a multitude of rivers alluded to in the conversation. One of the washerwomen complains: "My wrists are wrusty rubbing the mouldaw stains. And the dneepers of wet and the gangres of sin in it." The moldy stains she has to rub come from the Prague river then known as the Moldau, now called the Vitava, and the clothes are stained by the Russian Dnieper and the Ganges river of India.

The themes of the washerwomen's story of ALP are familiar to us from previous episodes, telling of a wife whose husband is in trouble and who scavanges gifts for her needy children. "And how long was he under loch and neagh?" (196) one of the women asks, wondering how long the HCE figure was under lock and key or under water in a Scottish loch. But the husband is also given credit for having worked hard to earn his "staly bread" by "this wet of his prow" (198). In turn, the ALP figure is described once again as cooking him breakfast with "blooms of fisk," "meddery eygs," and "staynish beacons on toasc," with "Greenland's tay" and "Kaffue mokau" (199). According to Roland McHugh's *Annotations to 'Finnegans Wake*, the "Tay," "Kafue," and "Mokau" are also rivers as well as tea, coffee, and mocha (199).

It is not clear how many children ALP had, with some saying it was "a hundred eleven," which may be why she "can't remember half of the cradlenames she smacked on them" (201). Various accounts are given of her first love experiences, one of them involving a priest who "plunged both of his newly anointed hands" into the cool waters of a stream, parting the "saffron strumans of hair, parting them and soothing her and mingling it," as though the river in which he washes his hands is indeed a young female Liffey (203). Joyce equates strands of hair with the steams of water in a river, and so when ALP is described enjoying her morning bath, we are told "First she let her hair fal and down it flussed to her feet its teviots winding coils" (206). She then "wove a garland for her hair" of "meadowgrass and riverflags, the bulrush and waterweed," and she adorned herself with jewelry made of "pattering pebbles and rumbledown rubble" (207). ALP then gets on her way to care for her family, and "like Santa Claus at the cree of the pale and puny" she responds to the needs of her children, "nistling to hear for their tiny hearties, her arms encircling Isolabella, then running with reconciled Romas and Rheims," then "bathing Dirty Hans' spatters with spittle, with a Christmas box apiece for aisch and iveryone of her childer" (209).

The washerwomen have now been talking for quite a while and it is getting late. One complains of a backache, "O, my back, my back, my bach," with "Bach" the German word for a brook. It is time to "Wring out the clothes! Wring in the dew!" The clothes have to be spread out to dry, "Spread on your bank and I'll spread mine on mine." They "lay a few stones on the hostel sheets," and hold "[s]ix shifts" and "ten kerchiefs" to the fire to dry (213). But the lateness of the hour also applies to their time of life as they are getting old and failing. "Can't hear the waters of," one of them says, and "My foos won't moos," complains the other, "I feel as old as yonder elm" (215). Despite the tiredness, they continue to talk: "Who were Shem and Shaun the living sons or daughters of?" But now it is "Night! Night!" (216) and so their conversation comes to an end.

Book II

Campbell and Robinson call Book II "The Book of the Sons," but it could also be called "The Book of the Children" since Issy and a small cohort of girls will also play a role in the various chapters.

The first chapter begins with a children's play, not a game but a theatrical performance titled *The Mime of Mick, Nick and the Maggies* and offering a list of characters that includes GLUGG (Shem), THE FLORAS, IZOD (Issy), CHUFF (Shaun), ANN (ALP), HUMP (HCE), some CUSTOMERS (possibly of a tavern), and SAUNDERSON and KATE, who may work at the pub (219-221). The time of the play is given as the present, and there will be settings, songs, and props.

The play begins by identifying Chuff as a sword-carrying angel ("Chuffy was a nangel then and his soard fleshed light like likening"), while Glugg is identified as a devil figure, "sbuffing and sputing" and "whipping his eyesoult and gnatsching his teats." The "first girly stirs" come on the scene flittering like insects or birds, "with zitterings of flight released and twinglings of twitchbells," making the air "shimmershake" (222). Soon a guessing game begins that Joyce identified in a letter as "Angels and Devils or colours," as John Bishop reminds us in his book (237). In the game, the children form two groups and confront each other ("they are met, face a facing. They are set, force to force") and ask each other questions ("A space. Who are you? A cat's mother. A time. What do you lack? The look of a queen") (223).

We are reminded of the "Nausicaa" chapter in *Ulysses*, where twin boys quarrel as they play on the beach, while their sister and her girlfriends watch. Glugg, "the poor one" who does not do well in the game, is reminiscent of little Tommy Caffrey, and both boys respond poorly to questions posed by their sister. When the girls in "Nausicaa" jokingly ask Tommy which of them is his sweetheart, he tearfully answers "Nao" three times (*Ulysses* 285). When Glugg is asked three questions in the *Wake*, he also answers "No" three times, and it becomes clear that "He has lost" while Chuff, surrounded by the girls, is in his heaven and feels all's right in the world ("Chuffchuff's inners even. All's rice with their whorl" (225). The girls continue to dance around Chuff, "So and so, toe by toe, to and fro they go round," and "they leap so looply, looply, as they link to light" (226). Meanwhile, Glugg goes off in desperation, finally deciding that the best thing he can do is to become a writer and join the Society of Authors, "Go in for scribenery with the satiety of arthurs," and write something on the order of "Ukalepe" or *Ulysses*. He even appears to echo the titles of various chapters in *Ulysses* such as "Loathers' leave" ("Lotus-Eaters"), "Had Days" ("Hades), "Skilly and Carubdish" (Scylla and Charybdis"), "A Wondering Wreck" ("Wandering Rocks"), and "Naughtsycalves" ("Nausicaa")" (229). "Nausicaa" will indeed surface again a few pages later when Glugg is once again asked a series of three questions, and this time gives answers even closer to Tommy Caffrey's: "Nao," "Naohao," and "Naohaohao" (233).

For the next 20-plus pages of the chapter, these themes, established at the beginning, will continue, with poor Glugg struggling and spurned by the girls while they praise Chuff ("You are pure. You are pure. You are in your puerity") (237). Not surprisingly, religion, prayers, and hymns are evoked since their games have cast them as angels and devils. "Hymnumber twentynine. O, the singing!" is announced, as the "Happy little girlycums" have "come to chant en chor" (234). Soon it becomes dark, and there is a call for "Lights, pageboy, lights!" (245), but the games continue until finally the play comes to an end with applause. "Upploud! The play thou schouwburgst, Game, here endeth. The curtain drops by deep request" (257), we are told, and the children go home: "Now have thy children entered into their habitations" (258).

Right at the opening of the second chapter of Book II we can see a dramatic change in the style of this episode—reminiscent of the changes with their newspaper headlines that mark the "Aeolus" chapter in *Ulysses*. Here the text takes a scholarly turn with marginalia on both the right and the left side, as well as footnotes at the bottom of each page. The marginalia offer comments by the brothers, each on one side, and changing places about midway through the chapter, while the footnotes give us their sister's observations. This layout accords with the theme of what is sometimes called "the homework chapter," or "Triv and Quad," as Campbell and Robinson refer to it (162). The chapter text suggests the form of a scholarly article, although presumably more advanced than one read by schoolboys for homework.

While the children work upstairs, their father appears to be downstairs serving customers in a pub. The chapter's beginning gives us little information but many questions. "As we there are where are we," it begins (260), and proceeds to refer to a "he" who is not clearly identified but who prompts a series of questions, "Who is he? Whose is he? Why is he? Howmuch is he? Which is he? When is he? Where is he?" and "How is he?" (261).

In their book *Understanding 'Finnegans Wake,'* Danis Rose and John O'Hanlon describe the first section of the narrative as taking the reader on a geographical journey (147), and, indeed, we appear to be led past a river, perhaps Dublin's or "Eblinn water," to a "phantom city" with a lovely vista "buona the vista," orchards, and the "creepered tower of a church of Ereland" (264). We may be passing through Phoenix Park, where we see "the phoenix, his pyre, is still flaming away with trueprattight spirit," until we find ourselves in Chapelizod outside of Dublin since we have come to "Izolde, her chaplet gardens" with their "hedges of ivy and hollywood and bower of mistletoe" (265).

The focus now shifts to the household of Shem and Shaun, the "jemmijohns" who work on some "rhythmatick" and pore over "Browne and Nolan's divisional tables" while their sister "will sit and knit on solfa sofa." (Brown & Nolan were Dublin publishers) (268).

From arithmetic, the boys' study will progress to many other subjects such as history, including "memoiries of Hireling's puny wars" or Ireland's Punic Wars (270), and to periods both B.C. and A.D. "Please stop if you're a B.C. minding missy, please do. But should you prefer A.D. stepplease" (272). The right margin next to this last comment refers to a "PANOPTICAL PURVIEW OF POLITICAL PROGRESS AND THE FUTURE PRESENTATION OF THE PAST," a not illogical description of the task of history.

A few pages later, as the right margin announces, we come to an intermission or recess—"INCIPIT INTERMISSIO" (278)—and thoughts soon turn from war to sports, "Since alls war that end war let sports be leisure and bring and buy fair. Ah ah athclete, blest your bally bathfeet" (279). But at this point Issy, who has been adding brief footnotes to the commentary, offers one that is almost a page long, beginning with suicidal thoughts ("I was thinking fairly killing times of putting an end to myself and my malody"). But then, she goes on to tout her own educational ambitions ("we will conjugate together") and ("I'll get my decree") because "I learned all the runes of the gamest game ever from my old nourse Asa" (279).

The "homework" chapter encompasses many areas of knowledge, as it concedes near the end, "We've had our day at triv and quad and writ our bit as intermidgets. Art, literature, politics, economy, chemistry, humanity, &c." (306). But the most dramatic moment in all these learning exercises comes on page 293, when a geometry lesson is supplemented by a diagram generally interpreted as an image of the mother's private parts as viewed by her sons. There is no mistaking that the diagram refers to ALP since the letters are clearly printed to represent what appears to form a sexual triangle. The concept of children's interest in their parents' sexuality is at the heart of Freud's concept of the "primal scene," the notion that children either remember or fantasize about parental copulation as a way of understanding their origins. In the *Wake* too, the scene is less erotic or bawdy than evocative of the dream compulsion to return to and understand beginnings, hence the many allusions throughout the book to Adam and Eve, the Garden of Eden, and Noah's flood. Here, just below the diagram, some of these biblical themes are evoked, with a reference to "Sare Isaac's" reminding us of Isaac as the biblical father of twins, and a reference to Genesis where "Eve takes fall".

We can therefore construe this moment in the episode to enlarge the notion of the twin boys' search for knowledge to include a desire to explore where they came from, which inevitably requires thinking of the womb and their mother's body. The marginal note on the left just under the ALP diagram alludes to "*Uteralterance or the Interplay of Bones in the Womb*" (293). And a few pages later one of the brothers appears to promise, or threaten, the other that "I'll make you to see figuratleavely the whome of your eternal geomater" (296). But even during this intimate joint visual adventure, the brothers remain at odds: "And Kev was wreathed with his pother" (303).

The end of the chapter, however, seems to offer something like graduation after all these lessons—"Commencement Day is at hand," Campbell and Robinson note (192). In honor of the occasion, the boys appear to be offered a "Noblett's surprize," or Nobel Prize, by their sugar daddy, "Heavysciusgardaddy, parent who offers sweetmeats" (306). The chapter ends with a long series of examination questions that might have been derived from an equally long list of italicized classical figures on the left margin. *Pericles*, for example, follows *Julius Caesar* in the margin, and appears to be accompanied by the question "Is the Pen Mightier than the Sword?"— perhaps an allusion to the fact that, like Caesar, he not only led Athens in the Persian wars, but also promoted oratory and the arts. *Lucretius*, the Roman poet and philosopher who wrote "On the Nature of Things," is linked to the topic of "The Uses and Abuses of Insects" (306), and *Tiresius*, whom the goddess Hera had turned into a woman for killing copulating snakes, raises the question "Is the Co-education of Animus and Anima Wholly Desirable?" (307).

The chapter ends with a set of visual images, including a figure thumbing its nose and a set of cross bows, or "crossbuns," according to Issy's footnote. There is also a charming NIGHTLETTER offering yuletide greetings to "Pep and Memmy," "wishing them all very merry Incarnations" and prosperity, or at least "plenty of preprosterousness" in their "coming new yonks." The letter is signed by "jake, jack and little sousoucie (the babes that mean too)" (308).

Chapter 3 of Book II leaves the children behind and returns to the father and the stories of his assorted problems. If we were to try to configure the scene domestically, we could picture ourselves leaving the children upstairs to return to the tavern downstairs, where men are drinking and talking and telling stories of various conflicts. The scene could be considered comparable in some respects to the "Cyclops" chapter of *Ulysses*, which is also set in a tavern with lively discussions by and conflicts among the customers.

But an interesting difference in this chapter concerns the role of media. Right from the beginning we are told that a radio is broadcasting, a "high fidelity dialdialler, as modern as tomorrow afternoon." We learn that it is equipped with "supershielded umbrella antennas for distance getting," and connected by magnetic links with "a vitaltone speaker, capable of capturing skybuddies, harbour craft emittences, key clickings, vaticum cleaners" (309), thereby producing a cacophony of sounds. The problem, as Rose and O'Hanlon point out, is that "though a radio programme is being broadcast, this is also an account of actual events in a public house, these two factors being virtually indistinguishable" (165).

Either in the pub, or on the air, a number of stories will be narrated. The first one concerns a hunchbacked and possibly Norwegian sailor whose "Hump! Hump!" (312) may identify him with Humphrey Chimpden Earwicker or HCE, who asks a "ship's husband" or shipping agent where he could order a suit of clothes. He is referred to a tailor named Kersse, who makes the suit which does not fit—because of the hump, the tailor claims—and leads to a furious confrontation with Kersse being called "you scum of a botch" and "you suck of a thick" (322). The radio broadcast interrupts with a "Welter focussed" or weather forecast, predicting "Wind from the nordth," as well as an "allexpected depression," "veirying precipitation," an "unusuable suite of clouds" "a retch of low pleasure," and an "outlook for tomarry." This last reference suggests that if one wanted to marry tomorrow, it would be with good visibility, "his ability good" (324).

Joyce scholar John Gordon does indeed find a marriage theme buried in this story: "That the sailor should send someone named a 'husband' to negotiate his 'suit' indicates that the tailor's daughter, the young ALP, is the object of the negotiation" (198), although an allusion to the "nowedding captain" (325) suggests that a marriage may not work out. At the heart of this chapter we hear a story now generally identified as "How Buckley Shot the Russian General," which critic Finn Fordham calls "one of the densest pieces of writing in one of the densest darkest parts of one of the densest darkest novels" (*Lots of Fun at 'Finnegans Wake'* 89).

Fordham notes that Joyce's father may have told his son this story about an Irish soldier in the Crimean War, who was about to shoot a Russian General when he noticed that he was defecating. The humanity of the moment made him hesitate, but when the General wiped himself with a bit of turf, the soldier was disgusted and shot him. In the *Wake*, this story is narrated by two figures named Butt and Taff, versions of Shem and Shaun, who may be regarded as radio comics, for, as Fordham notes, their scene "has often been understood as a dialogue that is taking place on television" (90), a medium apparently existing in crude experimental forms as early as the late 1920s, making it possible that Joyce had heard about it.

By introducing the notion that various accounts in this chapter are products of media, the continual interruptions and introductions of new topics become more understandable and justified. Butt and Taff's account is interrupted at one point by radio or television ("*verbivocovisual*") reporting a horse race, "*given by* The Irish Race and World": "*The huddled and aliven stablecrashers have shared fleetfooted enthusiasm with the paddocks dare and ditches*" (341). We are reminded here of the role that the Gold Cup race plays in *Ulysses*, and particularly in the "Cyclops" episode where Bloom gets in trouble because Lenehan mistakenly tells the fellows in the pub that Bloom has gone to collect his winnings, which he will presumably not share by standing drinks. In the *Wake* too, there will be a lot of betting and tipping reminiscent of the names of Butt and Taff: "*This eeriedreme has being effered you by Bett and Tipp. Tipp and Bett, our swapstick quackchancers*" (342).

The Butt and Taff dialogue goes on and on until at last Butt finishes the story in the first person, his name now relating more clearly to the Russian General's final action of "beheaving up that sob of tunf" in order to "wollpimsolff" or wipe himself in his "exitous erseroyal," presumably his royal butt. Buckley is outraged at the insult to Ireland, and "[a]t that instullt to Igorladns" he "gave one dobblenotch and I ups with my crozzier" to "cockshock rockrogn," in an allusion to the nursery rhyme, "Who Killed Cock Robin" (353). Buckley has shot the Russian General, an act that triggers the "*abnihilisation of the etym,*" that is, the annihilation of the atom or of the word, a dramatic event with all the predictive features of a nuclear explosion. We are told that it "*expolodotonates through Parsuralia with an ivanmorinthorrorumble fragoromboassity amidwhiches general uttermosts confussion are perceivable moletons skaping with mulicules,*" an explosion with an even more horrible rumble amid whose utter confusion, or nuclear fusion, we can perceive molecules escaping.

It may seem impossible that Joyce would have been aware of the concept of an atomic bomb before *Finnegans Wake* was published in 1939, but it turns out that H.G. Wells published a novel as early as 1914 called *The World Set Free*, which predicts a nuclear explosion. The Wikipedia article on Wells' novel explains that scientists at that time were already aware that "the slow natural radioactive decay of elements like radium continues for thousands of years, and while the rate of energy release is negligible, the total amount released is huge." Joyce was likely aware of this scientific thinking because he described a scenario similar to a nuclear explosion: "*projectilised from Hullullullu, Bawlawayo, empyreal Rome, and mordern Atems,*" or projected from Honolulu, Borneo, imperial Rome, and modern Athens, or modern atoms (353).

The Butt and Taff dialogue comes to an end, and the scene returns to the tavern whose customers argue about the conflict they just heard on the radio. "Shutmup," one says, defending Buckley, "And bud did down well right" (355). The tavern-keeper seems to adopt a positive note and tells an anecdote about reading a book with his "naked I" while visiting an outhouse "for relieving purposes in our trurally virvir vergitabale (garden)" (357)—a scene reminiscent of Bloom in the "Calypso" chapter of *Ulysses* reading a story in a penny-weekly magazine while sitting in the outhouse in his garden. The HCE figure appears to like the "(suppressed) book" he is reading, finding it "eminently legligible" and commending the quality of the paper. He claims to have read enough of it to hope "it will cocommend the widest circulation and a reputation coextensive with its merits when inthrusted into safe and pious hands" (356), an excellent review Joyce might have wished for his own suppressed books. He even commends the illustrations of "Mr Aubeyron Birdslay" (357)—a reference to Aubrey Beardsley, the English illustrator of Oscar Wilde's *Salome*.

Soon another radio interruption, possibly from a "ham" radio, tells us that we have just "beamed listening" to an excerpt from "John Whiston's fiveaxled production, *The Coach With The Six Insides*," to be continued in "*Fearson's Nightly*," perhaps a magazine like *Pearson's Weekly* (359). This is followed by a musical interlude beginning with the "dewfolded song of the naughtingels" or nightingales—possibly a reference to the Crimean War nurse Florence Nightingale ("floflo floreflorence") or the Swedish Nightingale ("sweetishsad lightandgayle"), the nickname of the Swedish singer Jenny Lind. More allusions follow to a series of composers. They include Meyerbeer ("meer Bare"), Bellini ("Bill Heeny"), Mercadante ("Smirky Dainty"), Beethoven ("beethoken"), and others, including Mozart ("sweetmoztheart") (359-360). "May song it flourish," the narrative voice tells us, and given the musical quality of much of the *Wake*'s prose, we may agree.

The remainder of the chapter will revisit the sins of the father, who at one point offers a confession of his sins although he complains about his accusers—"The rebald danger with they who would bare whiteness against me I dismissem from the mind of good" (364). HCE is nonetheless tried by a jury consisting of the people in the tavern, including four elders who are eventually identified with the four evangelists in the gospels, Matthew, Mark, Luke, and John ("Mr Justician Matthews and Mr Justician Marks and Mr Justician Luk de Luc and Mr Justinian Johnston-Johnson" (377). They claim that HCE should be ashamed of himself: "He should be ashaped of hempshelves, hiding that shepe in his goat," presumably for hiding a sheep in his coat (373). Other charges are levied, "Sell him a breach contact, the vendoror, the buylawyer" (374) and threats made: "Wait till they send you to sleep, scowpow. By jurors' cruces" (375).

The chapter ends with the tavern closing for the night while the tavern-keeper, described as plagued by a "wonderful midnight thirst" goes around to finish drinks his customers had left behind, ready to "suck up" "whatever surplus rotgut, sorra much, was left by the lazy lousers of maltknights and beerchurls in the different bottoms of the various different replenquished drinking utensils left there behind them on the premisses" (381). Not surprisingly he "came acrash", falls down, and in the end "he just slumped to throne" (382).

Chapter 4, the last chapter of Book II, begins with the sound of seagulls announcing its theme: The sea voyage of Tristan and Isolde, the betrayal of Tristan's uncle and Isolde's destined husband, King Mark, and the voyeuristic viewing and account of four old men identified with the four evangelists of the Bible. Scholar John Gordon, who makes efforts to put Wakean scenes into a plausible novelistic context, suggests we view it from the perspective of HCE in bed, with four bed posts looking down on him, remembering the romance of his youth (214). Campbell and Robinson offer a similar scenario: HCE's "body, helpless on the floor" represents King Mark of the Tristan myth dreaming "the honeymoon voyage of Tristram and Iseult" (248).

The chapter begins with the sound of birds mocking King Mark, "*Three quarks for Muster Mark!/ Sure he hasn't got much of a bark,*" and describing him as a rooster flapping out of Noah's ark. No longer the "*cock of the wark*" he is obliged to see that "*Tristy's the spry young spark/ That'll tread her and wed her and bed her and red her/ Without ever winking the tail of a feather.*" In the myth of Tristan and Isolde, Tristan is bringing Isolde to his uncle King Mark, who plans to wed her, but the couple falls in love on their voyage on the sea when they ingest a love potion. In Joyce's version, the four old men looking at the scene from above seem here identified with the birds "[o]verhoved, shrillgleescreaming. That song sang seaswans." The birds "trolled out rightbold when they smacked the big kuss," or saw the big kiss "of Trustan and Usolde" (383). Soon they are transformed from birds into men, "They were the big four, the four maaster waves of Erin," perhaps masts on the ship, "all listening, four," and identified with the evangelists, "Matt Gregory," "Marcus Lyons," "Luke Tarpey," and "old Johnny MacDougall." At this point they are described both as listening, "luistening and listening to the oceans of kissening," and looking "with their eyes glistening" as he (presumably Tristan) was "kiddling and cuddling and bunnyhugging scrumptious his colleen bawn" (384). Joyce's allusion to "The Colleen Bawn" refers to a play produced "in the good old bygone days of Dion Boucicault" (385), a 19th century Irish playwright who wrote and produced a work by that title that is more complex and sadder than the Tristan and Isolde story. Given the early reference to Noah's ark, and the fact that Tristan and Isolde's romance takes place on a ship at sea, it is not surprising that the evangelists will recount tales of drowning. "[T]here was the drowning of Pharoah and all his pedestrians and they were all completely drowned into the sea, the red sea" Johnny reports, and goes on to tell of "poor Merkin Cornyngwham, the official out of the castle on pension, when he was completely drowned off Erin Isles" (387). Campbell and Robinson believe this second allusion refers to Martin Cunningham in *Ulysses*, and it may suggest that perhaps he eventually dies by drowning (250). Later when "Matt Emeritus" speaks, he too will refer to "Poor Andrew Martin Cunningham!" (393). Like several earlier chapters, this one ends in a prayer ("*Anno Domini nostri sancti Jesu Christi*") and a song, possibly accompanied by musical instruments including "The Lambeg drum, the Lombog reed" and "the Lumbag fiferer" (398).

Book III

Like Book II, Book III also consists of four chapters. Some critics assume that these represent HCE, now in bed with his wife, dreaming about his sons with a particular focus on Shaun, and the first of the chapters will indeed include a long interrogation of Shaun.

A first-person voice begins by telling that "as I was dropping asleep" it heard the "peal of vixen's laughter among midnight's chimes from out the belfry of the cute old speckled church" (403) and that it saw in the "affluvial flowandflow" of water "garments of laundry" (404). This harks back to the earlier chapter of the washerwomen doing laundry in the stream. But the voice continues to say "as I was jogging along in a dream" it heard a high voice "echoating: Shaun! Shaun! Post the post!" As the clothing of the fellow Shaun is described in exacting detail, he does indeed appear to be a mailman since the initials "R.M.D.," which presumably stand for Royal Mail, Dublin (according to McHugh [404]), are seen embroidered on his shirt. Shaun is initially described as looking "grand, so fired smart, in much more than his usual health." But the voice also tells us that "[h]e was immense," and we soon learn that this is because "he had recruited his strength by meals of spadefuls of mounded food" that includes "half of a pint of becon," "a segment of riceplummy padding," "some cold forsoaken steak" and even more than this bacon, plum pudding, and steak (405). The list of his meals goes on and on, and it is therefore not surprising that he not only has a big heart, but "[t]hus thicker will he grow now, grew new. And better and better on butterand butter" (406).

After this description of Shaun as guilty of gluttony, the narrative voice is surprised to find that "I heard a voice, the voce of Shaun, vote of the Irish," and this will allow an interrogation of Shaun to now take place (407). Shaun begins the conversation by yawning and complaining that he is "exhaust as winded hare, utterly spent," and disgusted with the weight he has put on. He is after all a "mailman of peace," "the bearer extraordinary of these postoomany missive on his majesty's service," but perhaps this job should be performed by "my other," that is, his brother with whom he shared "the twin chamber," and who unlike himself, "looks rather thin, imitating me" (408). But as it is, his job will not be easy, given his excess weight and its effects on his knees and spine, "Fatiguing, very fatiguing. Hobos hornknees and the corveeture of my spine" (409). Shaun's interrogator addresses him in extraordinarily kind ways, calling him "honest Shaun," "Shaun honey" (410), "dear dogmestic Shaun" (411), "frank Shaun" (413), "[k]ind Shaun" (421), "Shaun illustrious" (422), and so on. Shaun responds in various moods, sometimes "naturally incensed" (412), and at other times apologetic. But his responses are often engaging, none more so than when he offers a "fable one, feeble too," of the "Ondt and the Gracehoper" (414), that we might recognize as the Aesop ("Esaup") fable of the Ant and the Grasshopper.

The charm of the telling of this fable lies to some extent in its poetic prose, but also in its entomological focus on insects. In the fable, the ant is the busy, hardworking creature collecting and saving resources for the winter, while the grasshopper plays and hops about without any thought of the hardships to come, which will force him to beg the ant for help in winter. Joyce, perhaps more spendthrift than miser, may have deliberately glossed himself in the description of the Gracehoper. "The Gracehoper was always jigging ajog, hoppy on akkant of his joyicity," we are told, while (unlike Joyce) "he was always making ungraceful overtures to Floh and Luse and Bienie and Vespatilla" to "commence insects with him," "even if only in chaste" (414). The Ondt, in contrast, seems to resemble the roomy-built and able-bodied ("raumybult and abelboobied") Shaun. He is "sullemn and chairmanlooking," unlike the "sillybilly of a Gracehoper" who "had jingled through a jungle of love and debts" and ends up with "[n]ot one pickopeck of muscowmoney to bag a tittlebits of beebread." Having saved nothing to buy food, the Gracehoper ends up wailing, "I am heartily hungry," and by the time winter comes he has eaten all the wallpaper along with everything else in the house, and is obliged to seek out the Ondt for help (416).

The Ondt, esconced on his throne, is "smolking a spatial brunt of Hosana cigals," and his special brand of Havana cigars are not the only thing that makes him "as appi as a oneysucker or a baskerboy on the Libido," given that the female insects, the flea "Floh", the louse "Luse," the bee "Bieni," and the little wasp "Vespatilla" are now serving him (417). The Gracehoper now offers a despairing concession to the Ondt in the form of a verse or a song. "*I forgive you, grondt Ondt, said the Gracehoper, weeping/ For their sukes of the sakes you are safe in whose keeping,*" and he adds, "*As I once played the piper I must now pay the count*" (418). The chapter ends by returning to Shaun's job as a postman and a letter that he carries: "*Letter, carried of Shaun, son of Hek, written of Shem, brother of Shaun, uttered for Alp, mother of Shem, for Hek, father of Shaun*" (420), and describes how he loses his balance ("lusosing the harmonical balance of his ballbearing extremities" [426]) and appears to fall into a barrel in a stream until he "spoorlessly disappaled and vanesshed" (427).

At the beginning of the next chapter, Book III chapter 2, Shaun seems to have survived his voyage in the barrel and returned ashore. He is now introduced as "Jaunty Jaun," and we are told that he is "amply altered for the brighter, though still the graven image of his squarer self as he was used to be, perspiring but happy" (429). He appears to have landed near a group of "twentynine hedge daughters out of Benent Saint Berched's national nightschool," who are "learning their antemeridian lesson of life" (430). They are "all barely in their typtap teens," and soon Shaun begins to deliver an extended sermon to them.

If there is a precedent to this chapter it may be found in Joyce's *A Portrait of the Artist as a Young Man,* where the teenage Stephen

Dedalus is subjected to a series of sermons at a religious school retreat that increasingly chastise him into a feeling of acute guilt and remorse for his sins. Jaun begins by specifically addressing his "Sister dearest" with "express cordiality" and "deep affection" (431). But he soon begins his moral lecturing, advising "Never miss your lostsomewhere mass," "Never hate mere pork which is bad for your knife of a good friday," "Never lose your heart away till you win his diamond back," among other strictures. Other rules follow, "First thou shalt not smile. Twice thou shalt not love. Lust, thou shalt not commix idolatry" (433), the last one somewhat changing the commandment not to commit adultery. Later he goes on to give advice on health and hygiene, telling them "you needed healthy physicking exorcise to flush your kidneys," urging them to be sportive and to eat well, perhaps spurred by his own propensity to overeat, "I never open momouth but I pack mefood in it." He does, of course, put his foot in his mouth, in a sense, when he lectures (437). He gives advice on reading, invoking children's literature like the nursery rhyme "Mary had a little lamb" ("I used to follow Mary Liddlelambe's flitsy tales"), but also saying that "Sifted science will do your arts good" (440).

A narrative voice at some point begins to talk about "hardworking Jaun" (441), but soon Jaun is back to address his "Sis dearest" in a "voise somewhit murky, what though still high fa luting" (448), and still giving instructions, "So now, I'll ask of you, let ye create no scenes in my poor primmafore's wake" (453). At one point he breaks into a "grand big blossy hearty stenorious laugh" that "hopped out of his woolly's throat like a ball lifted over the head of a deep field," presumably because "[s]omething of a sidesplitting nature must have occurred to westminstrel Jaunathaun" (454).

Now Issy (or "Tizzy") seems to respond with sweet nonsense to this sermon in her own inimitable way, "flushing but flashing from her dove and dart eyes as she tactilifully grapbed her male corrispondee to flusther sweet nunsongs in his quickturned ear." Her response has elements of confession: "I'm ashamed for my life," she tells him, perhaps for having left a "lost moment's gift of memento nosepaper," a newspaper or perhaps some tissues, at home (457). She appears to confess to pranks she played on "nurse Madge, my linkinglass girl, she's a fright, poor old dutch, in her sleeptalking when I paint the measles on her and mudstuskers to make her a man." "Issy done that, I confesh!" she admits (459).

She ends by offering to say one last little prayer before going to bed, "to thay one little player before doing to deed" (461). Shaun returns to say goodbye to her, perhaps with a lullaby," So gullaby, me poor Isley!" but promises to leave "my darling proxy" (462), presumably his twin brother, "Got by the one goat, suckled by the same nanna, one twitch, one nature makes us oldworld kin" (463). Still, he goes on and on before once more saying goodbye, "I hate to look at alarms, but, however they put on my watchcraft, must now close as I hearby hear by ear from by seeless socks 'tis time to be up and ambling" (468). Shaun's final departure is ambiguous and confused, and he may have pasted a bit of paper like a stamp on his brow, "he gummalicked the stickyback side and stamped the oval badge of belief to his agnelows brow," in a sense turning himself into a stamped letter (470). But whether he is mailed like a letter or simply runs off or sails off, he appears to be seen off by the girls waving to him "with a posse of tossing hankerwaves," and bidding him godspeed, "may the good people speed you, rural Haun" (471).

In the next chapter, Shaun has been transformed into "Yawn," and he is introduced as wailing, "Lowly, longly, a wail went forth. Pure Yawn lay low." We are told "His dream monologue was over, of cause, but his drama parapolylogic had yet to be, affact." And so he continues to wail, "Yawn in a semiswoon lay awailing and (hooh!) what helpings of honeyful swoothead (phew!), which earpiercing dulcitude."

His new trial will consist of a series of lengthy interrogations by "senators four" (474), a new version of the four evangelists we encountered earlier and now named "Shanator Gregory," "Shanator Lyons," "Dr Shunadure Tarpey," and "old Shunny MacShunny, MacDougal" (475). We have encountered interrogations before, and these, like earlier ones, will yield little information. "—Y?" a question begins, and the answer "—Before You!" makes it unclear whether the discussion is about alphabetical letters or about "why," asking for the cause of something (477). Campbell and Robinson suggest that "During the next pages Shaun will be put under terrific pressure by his examiners," but he will resist answering "with every dodge and artifice." "He evades with indirections and sophistries, pretends that he cannot speak English, and seizes upon irrelevant aspects of the question under discussion" (295). We get an example of this on page 485 when Yawn claims "Me no angly mo, me speakee Yellman's lingas."

Not surprisingly, since Shaun is a postman, some of the questions concern the letter that crops up repeatedly in discussions. "That letter selfpenned to one's other, that neverperfect everplanned?" someone asks, and is given the reply, "This nonday diary, this allnights newseryreel." (489). Rose and O'Hanlon suggest that Yawn, "lying at the centre of Ireland" may represent both a dump, like the midden heap introduced in earlier chapters, or "a kind of letter-box. Having enveloped and stamped himself in III.2, Shaun now appears to be his own mailbox, containing himself" (244). But at another point a letter appears to have come from ALP, since it is signed "Respect. S.V.P. Your wife. Amn. Anm. Amm. Ann" and thereby presumably addressed to HCE rather than Shaun (495).

Later, it is "Iscappellas" or Issy who seems to speak, possibly to herself: "Of course I know you are a viry vikid girl to go in the dreemplace and at that time of the draym." She goes on to report, "The boys on the corner were talking too," and appears to make an allusion to menstruation, when "your soreful miseries first come on you. Still to forgive it, divine my lickle wiffey, and everybody knows you do look lovely in your invinsibles" (527). Issy also appears to be identified with Alice in Wonderland, perhaps seen in the looking-glass, "Alicious, twinstreams, twinestraines, through alluring glass or alas in jumboland" (528).

The ending of this chapter is extremely confusing, because the four old evangelists seem to be replaced by a younger group that Campbell and Robinson refer to as the Brain Trust (320) based on their own claims— "We bright young chaps of the brandnew braintrust are briefed here" (529)—as they appear to take over the questioning not of Shaun but of HCE who has now reemerged. It is as though the generations have been turned upside down once again. When HCE is interrogated, he offers a lengthy self-defense, claiming he is famous in the English-speaking world, "I am known throughout the world wherever my good Allenglisches Angleslachsen is spoken," and commended for his decency, "I think how our public at large appreciates it most highly from me that I am as cleanliving as could be" (532). And many pages later he ends by citing all the things he has done for the woman he married, "I pudd a name and wedlock boltoned round her the which to carry till her grave, my durdin dearly, Appia Lippia Pluviabilla" (548). He also boasts that "I fed her," and lists such items as "spiceries for her garbage breath," "shains of garleeks and swinespepper," "gothakrauts," as well as "pudding, bready and nutalled and potted fleshmeats" (550). And he provided a lovely home for her, "I planted for my own hot lisbing lass a quickset vineyard and I fenced it about with huge Chesterfield elms and Kentish hops and rigs of barlow and bowery nooks and greenwished villas" (553).

It is unclear how he is judged by his listeners, but the chapter ends by reporting that his wife appeared to accept his gifts with "pleashadure," and that "she lalaughed." And so, apparently, did the four evangelists, "Mattahah! Marahah! Luahah! Joahanahanahana!" (554).

Campbell and Robinson call the fourth and last chapter of Book III "HCE and ALP—Their Bed of Trial." This section does indeed focus on the family with particular interest in the parents. If we were to think of Book III in narrative terms, we could imagine the earlier chapters having the parents downstairs, with the father working in the tavern, while the children are upstairs playing games and doing their homework. Now, however, it is nighttime, and the parents have gone to their bedroom and are in bed, possibly making love, until they are disturbed by a child, or children, having awakened, and possibly seeing the parents in their activities. This may all still be a dream, of course, as the chapter begins by asking "What was thaas?" and suggesting tumultuous sleep, perhaps, "Too mult sleepth. Let sleepth" (555). The parents may be in bed—"while kinderwardens minded their twinsbed"—with the four watchful evangelists now occupying the position of bedposts. Or the parents may be looking in on their twins who are now given the names of Kevin (probably Shaun, the "nicechild" who will be "commandeering chief of the choirboys' brigade the moment he grew up") and Jerry—Shem—described as the "badbrat" (555). Their sister, the "infantina Isobel" is described as possibly taking the veil when she grows up, to become a "beautiful presentation nun." She is clearly much loved, "the darling of my heart," and "so pretty, truth to tell, wildwood's eyes and primarose hair" as she "now evencalm lay sleeping" (556).

Although the beginning of the chapter is narrated, it offers the scene of the parents in the bedroom in theatrical language, describing the opening as a "Chamber scene. Boxed. Ordinary bedroom set. Salmonpapered walls," furnished with a "Chair for one. Woman's garments on chair. Man's trousers with crossbelt braces, collar on bedknob" (559). The theatrical description continues, announcing "Act: dumbshow/ Closeup. Leads." It then introduces the characters, "Man with nightcap, in bed, fore. Woman, with curlpins, hind. Discovered. Side point of view. First position of harmony" (559). The description of the house continues, noting the "chequered staircase" with "only one square step," and remarking "It is ideal residence for realtar" (560), suggesting that perhaps we have been given an overview not of a theatrical set, but of a realtor's tour.

Turning back to the family, they are now called the "Porters," "very nice people," with Mr. Porter "an excellent forefather" and Mrs.

Porter "a most kindhearted messmother" (560). There are two rooms upstairs housing the "little Porter babes." "Who sleeps in now number one, for example?" the narrative voice asks, and it turns out to be the little "noveletta and she is named Buttercup." "She is dadad's lottiest daughterpearl and brooder's cissiest auntybride" (561). Who sleeps in the second room, the speaker asks, and the answer is the "twobirds," presumably the brothers who are "so tightly tattached as two maggots to touch other." The first boy is likely to do well and eventually "wend him to Amorica to quest a cashy job" (562). But the other brother, "twined on codliverside, has been crying in his sleep," presumably because he is a "teething wretch" (563). In addition to teething, he has wet himself, or possibly spilled ink on himself from his fountain pen, "bespilled himself from his foundingpen as illspent from inkinghorn." He concedes that he writes a letter, "I write tintingface," possibly "steelwhite and blackmail." The weeping boy appears to get conflicting advice from mother and father, with the father telling him "Weeping shouldst thou not when man falls" (563), while the mother comforts him. "You were dreamend, dear," she tells him, "Sonly all in your imagination, dim. Poor little brittle magic nation, dim of mind" (565).

The chapter continues with the children possibly seeing the father's erection: "What do you show on? I show because I must see before my misfortune so a stark pointing pole" (566). Later, we get a narrative of utter indecency proposed by a "procurator Interrogarius" who presents a family caught up in degenerate behavior that includes "unnatural coits" and possibly incest, "Honophrius , Felicia, Eugenius and Jeremias are consanguineous to the lowest degree" (572). These are only imputations, not actual reports, and can therefore be construed as psychoanalytic fears or fantasies, since the parents appear to remain protective of their sleeping children, "While hovering dreamwings, folding around, will hide from fears my wee wee mannikin" and "guard my bairn" (576). The chapter continues for many more pages before ending with a "Tableau final" (590).

Book IV

Book IV consists of only a single chapter, the last one in the *Wake*, and is in some ways reminiscent of the last chapter of *Ulysses,* ending as it does with a woman's lyrical voice.

It begins with what appears to be a bright and sunny morning after an intense and difficult night, and with an invocation that reminds us of the beginning of the "Oxen of the Sun" episode in *Ulysses*, which is set in a maternity hospital and features a birth or beginning. The opening words "Sandhyas! Sandhyas! Sandhyas!" intone a Sanskrit prayer as well as the "Sanctus, Santus, Sanctus" of the Catholic mass. "The smog is lofting," we are told, there is a fine sun, "Sonne feine," and we hear a wake-up call, "Quake up, dim dusky." Dawn will bring a resurrection, "Array! Surrection" (593), after a night we might consider troubling, although later a voice asks "You mean to see we have been hadding a sound night's sleep?" and is answered, "You may so." The temperature has returned to normal and "Humid nature is feeling itself freely at ease with the all fresco" (597).

The horizon of this chapter appears greatly enlarged in the beginning, picturing a diverse Irish landscape and geography, and reintroducing figures—now also enlarged— that echo Earwicker family members, with the sons assuming mythic proportions as the ancient Irish saints Kevin and Patrick. Kevin is introduced as still admired by maidens—"A dweam of dose innocent dirly dirls. Keavn! Keavn!"—although they are here enumerated as a group of female saints. A reference to a "Kathlins" (601) may also allude to an incident in the life of the historical or mythical St. Kevin, who was allegedly admired by a maiden named Kathleen. "What does Coemghen?" (602) a narrative voice asks, invoking St. Kevin's Irish name of "Coemgen." A page or two later, it begins to narrate the story of "St. Kevin's bed," a period in the life of the saint when, wanting to live as an ascetic hermit, he made his home in a cave in Glendalough. In the *Wake*, St. Kevin builds a "rubric penitential honeybeehivehut in whose enclosure to live in fortitude" (605). He also excavated a space filled with water to function as a "hanbathtub" into which he immersed himself and experienced "with seraphic ardour the primal sacrament of baptism" (606).

However, we are reminded that this may still be part of the night's dream—"From sleep we are passing. Three. Into the wikeawades warld from sleep we are passing" (608), and soon we are back with the quarreling brothers reminiscent of Mutt and Jute in the first chapter. They are now given the Latin names *Muta* and *Juva* (609), and once again bring up a conflict between two men, this time a "fella Balkelly," perhaps an allusion to the Irish philosopher George Berkeley, and his opponent, "his mister guest Patholic," perhaps Saint Patrick (611). Their debate ends with the cry "God save Ireland," or rather "Good safe firelamp! hailed the heliots. Goldselforelump!" (613).

We are approaching the end of the chapter, and the end of the book, so it is reasonable to ask "How it ends?" (614). Not surprisingly, we will once more first get a letter seemingly found in a dump, like the earlier one, and once again written in the voice of ALP and addressed to "Dear. And we go on to Dirtdump. Reverend. May we add majesty?" and promising "Yon clouds will soon disappear looking forwards at a fine day" (615). Later she will announce an impending funeral, "The grand fooneral will now shortly occur. Remember. The remains must be removed before eaght hours shorp" (617). When the letter ends, she signs it "Alma Luvia, Pollabella" (619).

Her letter ended, ALP now begins her monologue, of sorts, first speaking seemingly to herself, "Soft morning, city! Lsp! I am leafy speafing," but then addressing a figure, her husband we assume, who does not appear capable of answering her. "Rise up, man of the hooths, you have slept so long!" she tells him, and urges him to get dressed, "Here is your shirt, the day one, come back. The stock, your collar. Also your double brogues" (619). "And stand up tall!" she tells him, "I want to see you looking fine for me" (620).

We might think this is an elderly couple, but when she says "The childher are still fast. There is no school today. Them boys is so contrairy" she suggests that this is either still a younger family with the twin sons we've encountered before, "one of him sighs or one of him cries," or a memory evoked from a past. And there is a girl as well, perhaps not as bright as her mother, "If she had only more matcher's wit" (620). Soon the couple is ready to go out, and although it is still very early, ALP thinks: "We've light enough. I won't take our laddy's lampern" (621). As they begin to walk, she takes his hand, "Come! Give me your great bearspaw," and now alludes to the fact that he appears unable to speak although he does respond to her, "But you understood, nodst? I always know by your brights and shades." Something is wrong with him, perhaps that fall from a ladder that we heard about in the early chapters, "[a]nd people thinks you missed the scaffold. Of fell design" (621).

As they go, she points out birds taking off, and soon they appear to be in the country, perhaps Howth, as Rose and O'Hanlon suggest (317), where they might visit the castle. "We might call on the Old Lord, what do you say? There's something tells me. He's a fine sport," she says, but warns her husband to "[r]emember to take off your white hat," while she too will remember to "drop my graciast kertssey" (623). She suggests that the Lord might even knight her husband or make him a magistrate, "He might knight you an Armor elsor daub you the first cheap magyerstrape," an idea that sounds more like fantasy than possibility. If this walk in the country can be thought to take place on Howth hill, then it very much harks back to Molly Bloom's last memory of the picnic on Howth on the day Leopold Bloom proposed to her, surrounded by nature in the country. ALP also remembers her husband's proposal, "How you said how you'd give me the keys of me heart. And we'd be married till delth to uspart." But then something happens and she says "But you're changing, acoolsha, you're changing from me, I can feel. Or is it me is?" (626).

And she is indeed changing as she appears to be coming to the end of her life. Soon she says, "I am passing out. O bitter ending!" And now her last journey begins, "And it's old and old it's sad and old it's sad and weary I go back to you, my cold father, my cold mad father, my cold mad feary father" (627–8). For a moment she wishes she were a child again, "Carry me along, taddy, like you done through the toy fair!"

The end is approaching, for ALP, and in the real world for James Joyce, who died less than three years after finishing his work. "End here. Us then. Finn, again!" and so *Finnegans Wake* ends with the words "A way a lone a last a loved a long the" and its last word is "the" (628).

6

Joyce's Legacy

What effect has Joyce's life and career had on our culture after his death and in our present day? It has been so huge that a comprehensive survey would require its own book. But I will begin with his influence on other writers, and then go on to consider films, music, journals, conferences, blogs and other evidence showing that Joyce continues to have a considerable impact on art and culture in the 21st century. These lists are partial at best, but they offer at least a glimpse of Joyce's enduring legacy.

The personal and literary footprint that Joyce had on writers he met or befriended is well known in the case of such figures as Ezra Pound, T. S. Eliot, and Ernest Hemingway, but it extended to other writers as well. Although she had both complimentary and unflattering things to say about Joyce's work, critics have noted that Virginia Woolf's 1925 *Mrs. Dalloway* recalls the narrative structure of *Ulysses*, with events set on a single day, and reflected in the language of interior monologues. Critic Morris Beja also found significant parallels in the experimental strategies of Woolf's 1931 novel, *The Waves* ("A World without *Ulysses*" 21). He also reported that William Faulkner was so in awe of Joyce that he was too nervous to speak to him when he saw him once on a trip to Europe in the 1920s. And F. Scott Fitzgerald "offered in Joyce's presence to jump out of a high window to show his reverence."

Some later writers cited or alluded to Joyce's work fairly explicitly. Anthony Burgess, the author of *A Clockwork Orange*, published an introduction to Joyce's work now available under the title *Re Joyce*, as well as a 1973 guide to *Finnegans Wake* titled *Joysprick*. He also wrote *Blooms of Dublin*, an operetta based on *Ulysses*, which aired on BBC radio to celebrate the centenary of Joyce's birth in 1982. The British playwright Tom Stoppard wrote a play in 1974 called *Travesties*, set in Zurich in 1917 when Joyce, Tristan Tzara, and Vladimir Lenin were all living there. Joyce also appeared as a fictional figure in Flann O'Brien's 1964 book, *The Dalkey Archive*, in which Joyce claimed that he had "published little." And allusions to a long black coat and a "Latin Quarter" hat reinforce the assumption of a Joyce reference in Samuel Beckett's 1980 "playlet" *Ohio Impromptu.*

Joyce's literary influence has continued into the 21st century. In 2003 the South African novelist J. M. Coetzee published a novel titled *Elizabeth Costello*, whose protagonist writes a book called *The House on Eccles Street* which retells the story of *Ulysses* from Molly Bloom's perspective. Critic Beja mentioned over 40 prominent authors who, in one way or another, had been influenced by Joyce's work. The list includes Jorge Luis Borges, Joyce Carol Oates, Norman Mailer, Salman Rushdie, and Vladimir Nabokov, who taught *Ulysses* during his tenure as a professor of Russian and European Literature at Cornell in the 1950s. The theorist Jacques Derrida wrote an essay about the significance of "Yes" in *Ulysses*. Finally, Joyce's work also had a surprising effect in the realm of physics. The physicist Murray Gell-Mann was scanning Joyce's *Finnegans Wake* when he ran across the word "quark" ("*Three quarks for Muster Mark*" 383). He subsequently used the term "quark" to identify an elementary particle that is a basic constituent of matter.

Given Joyce's efforts in 1909 to open Dublin's first movie house, the Volta Theatre, the transposition of his works into film is not at all surprising. Joyce even had a meeting with the famous film director Sergei Eisenstein in Paris in 1929, who drew comparisons between his 1925 film *Battleship Potemkin* and *Ulysses*. In 1967, the American filmmaker Joseph Strick released a black-and-white film titled *Ulysses*, starring Milo O'Shea and Barbara Jefford as Leopold and Molly Bloom. The movie was nominated for a Palme d'Or award at the Cannes Film Festival in 1967, where it ran into a surprising censorship problem which caused Strick to withdraw it from the competition (Margot Norris, *Ulysses* 27). Strick went on to make a film of Joyce's *A Portrait of the Artist as a Young Man* in 1977. Fionulla Flanagan, the actress who portrayed Gerty MacDowell in the 1967 Strick film, went on to make a movie called *James Joyce's Women* in 1983. A few years later, in 1987, the famous director John Huston made a movie based on Joyce's short story, "The Dead." It was his last film, and starred his daughter Anjelica Huston in the role of Gretta Conroy. In 2003, the Irish film-maker Sean Walsh also made a film of *Ulysses*, which was filmed in color and released with the title *Bloom*. It starred Stephen

Rea in the role of Leopold Bloom. And Pat Murphy produced a film titled *Nora* in 2000, which focused on Joyce's wife and starred Ewan McGregor as Joyce. But the most famous connection between Joyce and the world of cinema may be photographer Eve Arnold's iconic 1955 picture of Marilyn Monroe in a bathing suit at a playground, reading *Ulysses*. Arnold made it clear that this was not a stunt, and that Monroe apparently kept a copy of the book in her car and read it when she had time because "she loved the sound of it."

Music played a major role in all of Joyce's works. He had a beautiful voice and shared the stage of Dublin's Antient Concert Rooms with the tenor John McCormack (Beja 104), and in his later years, he promoted the career of another tenor, John Sullivan. It is therefore not surprising that Joyce's books have many allusions to music, beginning with the poems of "Chamber Music." Irish ballads also abound in his works, including the title of *Finnegans Wake*, based on an old Celtic folk song. Several of the stories in *Dubliners*—including "Clay," "A Mother," and "The Dead"—feature musical performances. The chapter "Sirens" in *Ulysses* is set in the Ormond Hotel, where there is singing and piano music in the background. And, of course, Molly Bloom is a singer about to go on a concert tour with her impresario and now lover, Hugh Boylan. In the course of these works a large number of songs are mentioned, which have come to play a significant role not only at Joyce conferences and special events on his birthday and on Bloomsday, but also in the cultural ambiance of Irish art. Author Zack Bowen published his *Musical Allusions in the Works of James Joyce* in 1974, noting that an earlier publication by Matthew Hodgart and Mabel Worthington "listed over 1000 songs in Joyce's works" (3). Many have been recorded and can now be downloaded on Amazon or heard on YouTube and Spotify Classical Playlists. They include a performance by tenor Kevin McDermott and pianist Ralph Richey titled *Music from the Works of James Joyce*. In 1991, Timothy Martin published *Joyce and Wagner,* in which he traces Joyce's interest in the composer's music, and adds an appendix of "Allusions to Wagner in Joyce's Work" (*Joyce and Wagner* 185-221). Critic Beja noted that Joyce also made his way into popular music. Bob Dylan's song "I Feel a Change Comin' On" contains the line "I've been reading James Joyce" (24). And the rock groups "Two Gallants" and "The Wading Girl" may have derived their names from Joyce's *Dubliners* and *Portrait.*

Academic interest in Joyce's work has always been strong and continues to grow and expand internationally. A number of journals offer regular publications of essays and notes on Joyce's work, as well as reviews of new publications and Joyce conferences. The University of Tulsa began publishing the *James Joyce Quarterly* in 1963, with Thomas F. Staley as its founder, and is currently edited by Sean Latham. In 2009, the University College Dublin Joyce Research Center and the National Library of Ireland began publishing the *Dublin James Joyce Journal* under the editorship of Luca Crispi and Anne Fogarty. Publications that focus chiefly on reviews include the *James Joyce Broadsheet*, published by the University of Leeds with Pieter Bekker, Richard Brown, and Alistair Stead as its editors. The University of Miami in Florida also publishes reviews in its issues of the *James Joyce Literary Supplement*, with Patrick McCarthy as its editor.

New York houses one of the oldest Joyce organizations in the country. Originally located in the Gotham Book Mart, the James Joyce Society opened in 1947, and its website claims T. S. Eliot as one of its first members. Other centers devoted to the study of Joyce have opened in various countries over the years. One of the most famous is the Zurich Joyce Foundation, operated by Fritz Senn, which opened in 1985. It has an extensive library of Joyce works, offers weekly discussion groups, as well as guest lectures. The James Joyce Italian Foundation began in 2008 and sponsors an Annual General Meeting in Rome in February. Also in Italy, the University of Trieste holds an annual Trieste Joyce School in the summer offering an array of speakers. There is an active James Joyce Society of Sweden and Finland, and Budapest in Hungary has also sponsored Joyce events in honor of Leopold Bloom's fictional ancestry. Joyce's work has received attention in Japan, Korea, and China. Scholar Eishiro Ito noted that an article on *A Portrait of the Artist as a Young Man* was published in a Japanese literary magazine in 1918, and Japanese translations of *Ulysses* began appearing in the early 1930s. The James Joyce Society of Japan is located at Tokoha University. Korea also has a James Joyce Society of Korea sponsored by Kookmin University, and Joyce's works, including *Finnegans Wake*, have been translated into Korean. A Chinese translation of *Ulysses* was produced in 1995, and a February 2013 issue of the *Guardian* published an article announcing the translation of *Finnegans Wake* into Chinese. "Bloomsday" celebrations in the week of June 16 are held, often annually, in many cities in the United States and Canada. Celebrations at the James Joyce Centre in Victoria, British Columbia have included a Bloomsday Photo contest, a digital publishing initiative involving *Ulysses*, and always much

Guinness ale. In recent years events of this kind have also been held in such cities as Pittsburgh, Syracuse, Spokane, and Montreal, as well as in Oslo, Madrid, Sydney and Melbourne in Australia, and Rio de Janeiro in Brazil. Of course, "Bloomsday" is a major annual event in Dublin, with lectures, musical and theatrical events, and tours around the city which trace the fictional journeys of Stephen Dedalus and Leopold Bloom on June 16, 1904. Finally, James Joyce Pubs can be found in cities around the world, including Athens, Madrid, Calgary, Lyon, and Istanbul.

The preceding list of Joyce's impact on writers, films, music, journals, translations, and literary societies is inevitably incomplete but points, nevertheless, to his influence on contemporary culture. An even more copious discussion of the popular legacy of *Ulysses*, in particular, can be found in Jonathan Goldman's piece titled "Afterlife" in *The Cambridge Companion to 'Ulysses.'* Additional venues for study and celebration can be found on weblogs or blogs, as they are now known, and there are a number that promote discussion of Joyce and his work. The *James Joyce Quarterly* sponsors an Academic Journal Blog, and *The Guardian* offers frequent articles on his work on its Books Blog. The New York Public Library blog posted a series of reviews of new books on Joyce on his birthday, February 2, 2016. In honor of Bloomsday, the "Scientific American" posted a piece titled "Ulysses by James Joyce, Greatest Mind-Scientist Ever" in 2013. The site titled "My Journey with James Joyce" presented an interesting discussion of "James Joyce on Management" in April of 2013, and Frank Delaney's site offers a podcast titled "Re: Joyce." On August 19, 2009, Richard Lewis posted a playful discussion titled "Reading James Joyce's *Ulysses* for the First Time." And "*Ulysses* on Tuesdays" offers quite detailed discussions of the work supplemented with images and links.

This particular means of encouraging informal online presentations and conversations about Joyce and his work will no doubt grow in the coming decades. And it offers additional evidence that Joyce's work has had a widespread effect on international culture not only in the 20th century, but also in the 21st. We can safely say there is no question that his significance will only continue to grow.

Suggested Reading

Armand, Louis. "*JJ/JLG.*" *Roll Away the Reel World: James Joyce and Cinema.* Ed. John McCourt. Cork: Cork University Press, 2010 (139–148). Armand discusses the effect of Joyce's work on such filmmakers as Jean-Luc Godard and Sergei Eisenstein.

Attridge, Derek. *Joyce Effects: On Language, Theory, History.* Cambridge: Cambridge University Press, 2000. This work explores how Joyce's texts challenge and influence the way we think about such topics as women's language, theory, and the power of literature.

Beja, Morris. *James Joyce: A Literary Life.* Columbus: Ohio State University Press, 1992. This compact biography offers a summary of the important moments of Joyce's life and relates them to the development and production of his literary works, along with the effects they produced on his reputation and fame.

Beja, Morris. "A World without *Ulysses.*" *A joyceful of talkatalka.* Eds. Raffaella Baccolini, Delia Chiaro, Chris Rundle, and Sam Whitsitt. Bologna: Bononia University Press, 2011. 19–27. Published in a volume dedicated to Rosa Maria Bollettieri Bosinelli, this essay discusses the influence of Joyce's work on other writers, as well as on popular culture.

Bishop, John. *Joyce's Book of the Dark: 'Finnegans Wake.'* Madison: The University of Wisconsin Press, 1986. In his detailed and comprehensive study of *Finnegans Wake,* Bishop explores the work as it delves into the experience of human consciousness in the night, in sleep, and in dream, with a particular focus on the ensuing effects of its language and its intellectual scope.

Bowen, Zack. *Musical Allusions in the Works of James Joyce.* Albany: State University of New York Press, 1974. Bowen begins by tracing musical allusions in Joyce's poetry, *Exiles, Dubliners, Stephen Hero,* and *A Portrait of the Artist as a Young Man.* But inevitably the major portion of this study is devoted to *Ulysses,* whose musical references and allusions he examines episode by episode from "Telemachus" to "Penelope."

Brivic, Sheldon. *Joyce the Creator.* **Madison: The University of Wisconsin Press, 1985.** Using the metaphor of God's mind, Brivic examines how Joyce projects himself into his texts through the multiplicity of voices he creates.

Brooker, Joseph. "Reception History." *The Cambridge Companion to 'Ulysses'.* **Ed. Sean Latham. Cambridge: Cambridge University Press, 2014.** This article begins with the production and publication history of *Ulysses,* including its obstacles and controversies. It then continues with a discussion of the book's various editions, and the critical response to its evolving appreciation and understanding.

Brown, Richard. *James Joyce and Sexuality.* **Cambridge: Cambridge University Press, 1985.** Brown looks at Joyce's views on marriage, on feminist dimensions in his work, and on the influence of modern perspectives on sexual divisions and difference.

Campbell, Joseph, and Henry Morton Robinson. *A Skeleton Key to 'Finnegans Wake.'* **New York: The Viking Press, 1969.** First published in 1944, only five years after Joyce's death, the *Skeleton Key* offers a systematic and detailed synopsis of each chapter of *Finnegans Wake,* presented in a clear and approachable way that makes the work accessible to readers.

Cheng, Vincent J. *Joyce, Race, and Empire.* **Cambridge: Cambridge University Press, 1995.** Born and raised in Ireland under British colonial rule, Joyce's awareness of the oppressions of colonialism work their way into his fictions in multiple and significant ways, as Cheng explores in this work.

Cheng, Vincent John. *Shakespeare and Joyce: A Study of 'Finnegans Wake.'* **University Park: The Pennsylvania State University Press, 1984.** The focus of this study is the influence of Shakespeare's work on *Finnegans Wake,* with details of Shakespearean motifs and allusions in the novel.

Crispi, Luca. *Joyce's Creative Process and the Construction of Characters in 'Ulysses.'* **Oxford: Oxford University Press, 2015.** This study explores how the characters in *Ulysses* were created and developed. Crispi explores notes, manuscripts, and other archival materials to demonstrate Joyce's strategies.

Davison, Neil R. ***James Joyce, 'Ulysses', and the Construction of Jewish Identity.*** **Cambridge: Cambridge University Press, 1998.** Given the significance of the Jewish Leopold Bloom as the protagonist of *Ulysses,* the question of Joyce's perception and representation of Jews in his literary works deserves the careful and complex exploration it receives in this book.

Devlin, Kimberly J. ***James Joyce's 'Fraudstuff'.*** **Gainesville: University Press of Florida, 2002.** Devlin explores how fraud is exhibited in the thoughts, actions, and suppressed emotions and desires of characters throughout Joyce's works.

Devlin, Kimberly J. ***Wandering and Return in 'Finnegans Wake'.*** **Princeton: Princeton University Press, 1991.** Invoking psychoanalytic and feminist theories, among others, this study demonstrates how Joyce draws on his earlier works to explore issues of identity, selfhood, and gender in *Finnegans Wake.*

Ellmann, Richard. ***James Joyce.*** **New and Revised Edition. Oxford: Oxford University Press, 1983.** Considered one of the great literary biographies of the 20th century, this work covers effectively every aspect of Joyce's life and supports its information with a wealth of material, including letters, documents, photographs, conversations, and detailed notes.

Feshbach, Sidney. "'Fallen on His Feet in Buenos Ayres': Frank in 'Eveline'." ***James Joyce Quarterly*** **20.2 (Winter 1983): 223–27.** With only a brief note, this piece disputes earlier constructions of the characters in Joyce's short story "Eveline" by looking at the issue of Irish emigration.

Fordham, Finn. ***Lots of Fun at 'Finnegans Wake': Unravelling Universals.*** **Oxford: Oxford University Press, 2007.** The question of how Joyce constructed *Finnegans Wake* is explored in this work by comparing different drafts of particular passages in the text that show how they changed, what Joyce retained and what he replaced, and how this process produced some of the work's intriguing complexities.

Gifford, Don, with Robert J. Seidman. ***'Ulysses' Annotated: Notes for James Joyce's 'Ulysses.*** **Revised and Expanded Edition. Berkeley: University of California Press, 1988.** This 637-page volume offers an encyclopedia of references in *Ulysses,* with descriptions and explanations of place names, historical and cultural figures, foreign phrases, slang terms, and much more. The study is considered an indispensable guide to Joyce's novel.

Gillespie, Michael Patrick. *Reading the Book of Himself: Narrative Strategies in the Works of James Joyce.* **Columbus: Ohio State University Press, 1989.** This exploration of how the texts in Joyce's works prompt and gesture to readers contains chapters on nearly all of Joyce's works, including *Stephen Hero* and his play *Exiles.*

Gordon, John. *Finnegans Wake: A Plot Summary.* **Dublin: Gill and Macmillan, 1986.** Rather than focusing on the experimentalism of *Finnegans Wake,* this study turns attention back to aspects of its realism, to time, place, characters, and events, by systematically looking at what happens in each chapter of the four Books in the work.

Groden, Michael. *'Ulysses' in Progress.* **Princeton: Princeton University Press, 1977.** This early study of the "prepublication" history of *Ulysses*—Joyce's writing process during the years of its production both in serial and in published forms—examines notebooks, drafts, manuscripts, typescripts and proof to elucidate Joyce's composition strategies.

Henke, Suzette. *Joyce and the Politics of Desire.* **New York: Routledge, 1990.** Henke presents a feminist assessment of Joyce's works using psychoanalytic theory with particular reference to the work of Sigmund Freud, Jacques Lacan, and Julia Kristeva.

Henke, Suzette and Elaine Unkeless, editors. *Women in Joyce.* **Urbana: University of Illinois Press, 1982.** This collection of essays looks at the diversity and vitality of women in Joye's works from a feminist perspective, covering a range from *Stephen Hero* to *Finnegans Wake.*

Herr, Cheryl. *Joyce's Anatomy of Culture.* **Urbana: University of Illinois Press, 1986.** Herr examines the influence of Irish popular culture in Joyce's works, including newspapers, theatrical performances in pantomime and music halls, and religious sermons.

Herring, Phillip F. ***Joyce's Uncertainty Principle.*** **Princeton: Princeton University Press, 1987.** This study examines how and why Joyce deliberately introduced ambiguity in many places in his work, making it difficult to determine whether the questions raised can be resolved or are destined to remain a mystery.

Joyce, James. *Collected Poems.* **New York: The Viking Press, 1969.** This slim volume contains Joyce's early poems published under the title of "Chamber Music," the poems he titled "Pomes Penyeach," and the single poem, "Ecce Puer," commemorating the birth of his grandson and the death of his father.

Joyce, James. *The Critical Writings of James Joyce,* **edited by Ellsworth Mason and Richard Ellmann. Ithaca, N.Y.: Cornell University Press, 1989.** Fifty-seven items written by Joyce are collected in this volume, including essays, letters to editors, lectures, discussions of such literary figures as Shakespeare, William Blake, and Oscar Wilde, and satirical poems.

Joyce, James. *Dubliners.* **Ed. Margot Norris. New York: W. W. Norton & Company, 2006.** The text of *Dubliners* in this book was edited by Hans Walter Gabler with Walter Hettche and begins with an "Introduction" by Gabler. The book also offers maps, photographs, musical scores, posters, and other materials, as well as a collection of eight critical essays by Joyce scholars on various stories in the volume.

Joyce, James. *Exiles.* **Mineola, N.Y.: Dover Publications, Inc., 2002.** *Exiles* is not the only play Joyce wrote, but it is the only one that has survived. It is thought to reflect some of Joyce's own experiences and those of his family during their early years abroad in Europe.

Joyce, James. *Finnegans Wake.* **New York: Penguin Books, 1967.** The volume contains all 628 pages of *Finnegans Wake*, but no other commentary or other materials.

James Joyce. *A Portrait of the Artist as a Young Man.* **Text, Criticism, and Notes. Edited by Chester G. Anderson. New York: Penguin Books, 1977.** The text of *A Portrait of the Artist as a Young Man* is supplemented by over 60 pages of "Explanatory Notes" at the end of this volume. It also offers a set of "Related Texts by Joyce," an array of critical commentary with essays from Joyce's own time, as well as from contemporary critics.

Joyce, James. ***Stephen Hero.*** **Ed. Theodore Spencer. New York: New Directions Publishing, 1963.** This edition of Joyce's early version of *A Portrait of the Artist as a Young Man* succeeds one first published in 1944, and offers a "Foreword" by John J. Slocum and Herbert Cahoon, as well as an "Introduction" by Theodore Spencer.

Joyce, James. ***Ulysses,*** **edited by Hans Walter Gabler with Wolfhard Steppe and Claus Melchior. New York: Vintage Books, 1986.** Generally referred to as "The Gabler Edition" of *Ulysses,* this work begins with a preface by Richard Ellmann and a foreword by Hans Walter Gabler, who also offers a brief "Note on the Text." The "Afterword" by Michael Groden discusses the challenges of the editing process of *Ulysses,* as well as the controversy that erupted around the publication of this volume.

Kenner, Hugh. "Molly's Masterstroke." ***James Joyce Quarterly*** **10, 1 (Fall 1972): 19–28.** Kenner's essay offers an intriguing and arguably controversial discussion of how Molly Bloom may have dealt with her affair with Hugh "Blazes" Boylan on June 16, 1904, in *Ulysses.*

Kenner, Hugh. ***Dublin's Joyce.*** **New York: Columbia University Press, 1987.** Ranging from the poems of "Chamber Music" to *FinnegansWake,* this study by one of the most distinguished critics of Joyce's works explores them as his responses to the culture and transformations of his native city.

Kershner, R. B. ***Joyce, Bakhtin, and Popular Literature.*** **Chapel Hill: The University of North Carolina Press, 1989.** Popular literature plays a prominent role in Joyce's writings, with many references to newspaper articles, romance novels, periodicals, children's adventure stories, and much more. Kershner discusses the significance of this wealth of material read by ordinary people in Joyce's stories and novels, using the work of the literary theorist Mikhail Bakhtin to explore its complicated functions.

Killeen, Terence. ***'Ulysses' Unbound: A Reader's Companion to James***

Joyce's 'Ulysses.' **Bray, Co. Wicklow: Wordwell Ltd., 2004.** The main focus of this work is to make Joyce's *Ulysses* more accessible by offering a commentary on each of the 18 episodes of the work, including a summary of events, discussion of the Homeric parallels and the style in which they are written, notes and a select glossary. In addition, there are brief sections on Joyce's life, the production of *Ulysses,* an afterword, a diagram of the schema, and a bibliography.

Lawrence, Karen. *The Odyssey of Style in 'Ulysses'.* **Princeton: Princeton University Press, 1981.** *Ulysses* is characterized by dramatic stylistic changes that transform the work and inevitably frustrate the reader's expectations. Lawrence tracks how these "protean transformations" gradually change narrative norms to parody and undermine the very concept of a narrative voice by looking at Joyce's most extreme stylistic experiments in the novel.

Martin, Timothy. *Joyce and Wagner: A Study of Influence.* **Cambridge: Cambridge University Press, 1991.** This work offers an analysis of Joyce's familiarity with, and interest in, the works of Richard Wagner, and their effect on Joyce's writing, which displays a large number of specific allusions to the composer's works.

McCarthy, Patrick A. *The Riddles of 'Finnegans Wake*. **Cranbury, N.J., Associated University Presses, Inc., 1980.** McCarthy calls *Finnegans Wake* "a giant riddle," but he also points to and explores specific riddles that are introduced and discussed in the work, such as the ones posed in the "Quiz" chapter, Shem's riddle "when is a man not a man," the prankquean's riddle, Izod's heliotrope riddle, and others.

McHugh, Roland. *Annotations to 'Finnegans Wake'.* **Baltimore: The Johns Hopkins University Press, 1991.** This major guidebook to *Finnegans Wake* allows readers to look up words in the work that puzzle them: foreign words, the names of persons, places, things, titles, literary allusions, myths, and much more. The book's pages correspond to the pages of the text of *Finnegans Wake,* and words are placed in the same order as in the *Wake* so that readers can easily look them up.

Mitchell, Breon. "*A Portrait* and the *Bildungsroman* Tradition." *Approaches to Joyce's 'Portrait'.* **Eds. Thomas F. Staley and Bernard Benstock. Pittsburgh: University of Pittsburgh Press, 1976.** Breon examines *Portrait* in light of the conventions of adolescent and artistic development displayed in the *Bildungsroman,* pointing out that the narrative innovations in this work, with its maturing style, enrich the genre itself.

Mullin, Katherine. "'Don't cry for me, Argentina': 'Eveline" and the seductions of emigration propaganda." *Semicolonial Joyce.* **Eds. Derek Attridge and Marjorie Howes. Cambridge: Cambridge University Press, 2000. 172–200.** Irish emigration is discussed in this essay as a fraught topic of propaganda in Irish history in the late 19th and early 20th century, which Joyce's story 'Eveline' evokes and resists amid the pressures and anxieties of the young protagonist's difficult decision.

Nadel, Ira B. *Joyce and the Jews: Culture and Texts.* **Gainesville: University Press of Florida, 1996.** Nadel's wide-ranging study of Joyce's affinity with Jews of his acquaintance and Judaic history and culture looks at a wide range of scholarly material to offer chapters on Jewish identity, typology, and Jewish cities as they relate to Joyce's work.

Norris, Margot. *Virgin and Veteran Readings of 'Ulysses'.* **New York: Palgrave Macmillan, 2011.** Imagining what it might be like to read *Ulysses* for the first time without any knowledge of the work allows Norris to uncover the considerable suspense and surprises that the text offers in its hidden narratives and subplots.

Norris, Margot. *Ulysses.* **Cork: Cork University Press, 2004.** The title refers to the 1967 Joseph Strick film of Joyce's *Ulysses,* and the book details the process of making the movie, along with the challenges involved in translating the text into a cinematic medium.

Parrinder, Patrick. *James Joyce.* **Cambridge: Cambridge University Press, 1984.** This survey of Joyce's work is committed to addressing all of his books, including his poetry, *Stephen Hero, Exiles, Giacomo Joyce,* as well as *Dubliners, Portrait, Ulysses,* and the *Wake,* while relating the texts to other writers and intellectuals.

Rose, Danis, and John O'Hanlon. *Understanding 'Finnegans Wake': A Guide to the Narrative of James Joyce's Masterpiece.* **New York: Garland Publishing, Inc., 1982.** This systematic journey through the text of *Finnegans Wake* uses a variety of strategies: narrating what is going on, summarizing, paraphrasing, interpreting, citing criticism, with the goal of making the work accessible and less daunting.

Schwaber, Paul. *The Cast of Characters: A Reading of 'Ulysses'.* **New Haven: Yale University Press, 1999.** As the title suggests, this study of *Ulysses* focuses on the characters in the work, both major and minor, but with particular attention to their inner lives—an approach enriched by Schwaber's experience as a psychoanalyst.

Scott, Bonnie Kime, editor. *New Alliances in Joyce Studies.* **Newark: University of Delaware Press, 1988.** Scott here offers a wide-ranging collection of essays collected in groups with such titles as "Recent Theory Applied to Joyce," "Analogies from Art," "Feminine Revisions," "Joyce and Other Women Writers," and "Textual Workshops," among others.

Senn, Fritz. *Joyce's Dislocutions: Essays on Reading and Translation,* **edited by John Paul Riquelme. Baltimore: The Johns Hopkins University Press, 1984.** In this important volume, Riquelme collects thirteen essays written by Fritz Senn over a period of more than a decade.

Sherry, Vincent. *James Joyce: 'Ulysses'.* **Cambridge: Cambridge University Press, 1994.** This book is part of what is described as a "textbook series," designed to serve as a guide to first-time readers of *Ulysses,* while nonetheless illuminating new perspectives for seasoned readers.

Shloss, Carol Loeb. *Lucia Joyce: To Dance in the Wake.* **New York: Farrar, Straus and Giroux, 2003.** This biography of Joyce's daughter supplements what is known about her life by considering materials and information that might have constructed a much fuller portrait of Lucia Joyce if they had been preserved.

Spinks, Lee. *James Joyce: A Critical Guide.* **Edinburgh: Edinburgh University Press, 2009.** A comprehensive and detailed study, this work offers a chapter on Joyce's life, commentary on each of the works from *Chamber Music* to *Finnegans Wake*, and a section on various critical approaches to the works, including feminist, psychoanalytic, and post-structuralist studies.

About the Author

Margot Norris, Chancellor's Professor of English and Comparative Literature at the University of California, Irvine prior to her retirement in 2011, specializes in early twentieth century literature, with a particular focus on the work of James Joyce. She served as president of the International James Joyce Foundation from 2004 to 2008, and is the author of numerous publications on Joyce. Her books include *The Decentered Universe of "Finnegans Wake"* (1976), *Joyce's Web: The Social Unraveling of Modernism* (1992), and *Virgin and Veteran Readings of "Ulysses"* (2011).

Afterword

Thank you for reading *Simply Joyce*!

If you enjoyed reading it, we would be grateful if you could help others discover and enjoy it too.

Please review it with your favorite book provider such as Amazon, BN, Kobo, iBooks or Goodreads, among others.

Again, thank you for your support and we look forward to offering you more great reads in the future.

A Note on the Type

Cardo is an Old Style font specifically designed for the needs of classicists, Biblical scholars, medievalists, and linguists. Created by David J. Perry, it was inspired by a typeface cut for the Renaissance printer Aldus Manutius that he first used to print Pietro Bembo's book *De Aetna*, which has been revived in modern times under several names.

CPSIA information can be obtained
at www.ICGtesting.com
Printed in the USA
LVOW07s0550020517
532923LV00001B/131/P